The Way of the Masks

CLAUDE LÉVI-STRAUSS

The Way of the Masks

Translated from the French
by
SYLVIA MODELSKI

UNIVERSITY OF WASHINGTON PRESS
Seattle

Library of Congress Cataloguing-in-Publication Data

Lévi-Strauss, Claude
   The way of the masks.
   Translation of: La voie des masques.
   Bibliography: p.
   Includes index.
   1. Indians of North America—Northwest coast of North America—Masks 2. Indians of North America—Northwest coast of North America—Art 3. Indians of North America—Northwest coast of North America—Religion and mythology I. Title.
E78.N78L4513   732'.2   82-2723   AACR2
ISBN 0-295-96636-X (pbk.)

Translator's Note

Voie, the French word for "way," is a homophone of *voix*, meaning "voice." Thus, the original title, *La Voie des masques*, is polysemous and not fully translatable into English.

In translating summaries of myths and other documents, rather than give a new version of the author's French rendition of the texts, I have retained, as far as possible, the wording of the original source.

For most Indian proper names, I have followed the author's spelling, which is based on different orthographies developed by anthropologists working in the Northwest around the turn of the century. The fact that ethnographers, studying different groups, phonetically transcribed the Indian words according to their individual orthographies, has led to a variety of spellings for a single name.

Several people have helped in preparing the English edition for publication. I wish to thank George MacDonald for choosing and providing illustrations for Part II, and Peter Macnair and Bill Holm, who gave helpful guidance with the maps and illustrations.

I am grateful to Professor Lévi-Strauss for the many suggestions he made to improve the translation, and for his generous response to all requests for clarification of the text.

Contents

Illustrations

The Way of the Masks

Part I

1

Enigma of a Mask

"There is in New York", I wrote in 1943, "a magic place where the dreams of childhood hold a rendezvous, where century-old tree trunks sing and speak, where indefinable objects watch out for the visitor, with the anxious stare of human faces, where animals of superhuman gentleness join their little paws like hands in prayer for the privilege of building the palace of the beaver for the chosen one, of guiding him to the realm of the seals, or of teaching him, with a mystic kiss, the language of the frog or the kingfisher. This place, on which outmoded but singularly effective museographic methods have conferred the additional allurements of the chiaroscuro of caves and the tottering heap of lost treasures, may be seen daily from ten to five o'clock at the American Museum of Natural History. It is the vast ground-floor gallery devoted to the Indians of the Pacific Northwest Coast, an area extending from Alaska to British Columbia.

"Surely it will not be long before we see the collections from this part of the world moved from ethnographic to fine arts museums to take their just place amidst the antiquities of Egypt or Persia and the works of medieval Europe. For this art is not unequal to the greatest, and, in the course of the century and a half of its history that is known to us, it has shown evidence of a superior diversity and has demonstrated apparently inexhaustible talents for renewal. . . .

"This century and a half saw the birth and flowering of not one but ten different art forms: from the hand-woven blankets of the Chilkat (a craft unknown in the region until the beginning of the nineteenth century), which immediately attained the highest perfection in textile art by using only sharp yellow extracted from moss, black drawn from cedar bark, and the coppery blue of mineral oxides, to the exquisite argillite sculptures given the high gloss of black obsidian (verging on the knickknack, they illustrate the flamboyant decadence that befalls an art suddenly in possession of steel tools, which in their turn destroy it), passing through the mad vogue, lasting only a few years, of dance headdresses emblazoned with carved faces set against a mother-of-pearl background and encircled with fur or white down from which ermine pelts cascade like curls. This unceasing renewal, this inventive assuredness that guarantees success wherever it is applied, this scorn for the beaten track, bring about ever new improvisations which infallibly lead to dazzling results—to get any idea of them, our times had to await the exceptional destiny of a Picasso. With this difference, however: that the daring feats of a single man, which have been taking our breath away for the past thirty years, were already known and practiced by a whole indigenous culture for one hundred and fifty years or even longer. For there is no reason for us to think that the development of this multiform art has not maintained the same rhythm since its remotest origins, which are still unknown. A few stone objects excavated in Alaska, however, prove that this powerfully idiosyncratic art—easily recognized in even its archaic form—dates from an ancient epoch, a phrase given here the relative value it must assume when applied to American archeology.

"At any rate, as late as the end of the nineteenth century, a rosary of villages was strewn along the coast and the islands, from the Gulf of Alaska to the southern tip of Vancouver Island. At their peak of prosperity, the Northwest Coast tribes may have numbered from 100,000 to 150,000 souls: a ridiculously low figure when one considers that the intensity of expression and important lessons of this art were worked out in their entirety in this remote province of the New World by a population whose density varied, according to the region, from 0.1 to 0.6 inhabitant per square kilometer. To the north were the Tlingit, to whom we owe sculptures of subtle and poetic inspiration and precious ornaments; then, toward the south, came the Haida with their monumental works, filled with vigor; next, the Tsimshian, who are their equals but with perhaps a more human sensibility; then, the Bella Coola, whose masks affect a stately style and in whose palette cobalt blue predominates; the Kwakiutl, with their unbridled imagination, who, in creating their dance masks, indulge in stupefying orgies of form and color; the Nootka,* restrained by a quieter realism; finally, in the extreme south, the Salish, whose much simplified style is angular and schematic—here, one loses track of the northern influence completely.

. . . .

"For the spectator at initiation rites, the dance masks (which opened suddenly like two shutters to reveal a second face, and sometimes a third one behind the second, each one imbued with mystery and austerity) were proofs of the omnipresence of the supernatural and the proliferation of myths. Upsetting the peace of everyday life, the masks' primal message retains so much power that even today the prophylactic insulation of the showcases fails to muffle its communication. Stroll for an hour or two across this hall so thick with 'living pillars.' By way of another correspon-

---

*The term "Nootka," applied by Captain James Cook to the people who occupy the west coast of Vancouver Island, has been replaced in current usage by "Westcoast" or "Nuu-Chah-Nulth."

Northwest Coast Indian Gallery of the American Museum of Natural History in 1943 (Courtesy, AMNH, 318931)

dence, the words of the poet* translate exactly the native term designating the sculptured posts used to support house beams: posts that are not so much things as living beings 'with friendly eyes,' since in days of doubt and torment, they too let out 'confused words,' guide the dweller of the house, advise and comfort him, and show him a way out of his difficulties. Even now, one would have to make an effort to recognize the dead tree trunks within the pillars and to remain deaf to their stifled voices; just as it would be difficult not to perceive, here and there behind the showcase glass, a sombre face, the 'Cannibal Raven' clapping its beak like wings, or the 'Master of the Tides' summoning forth the ebb and flow with a wink of its ingeniously articulated eyes.

"For nearly all these masks are simultaneously naive and ferocious mechanical contraptions. A system of ropes, pulleys, and hinges can cause mouths to mock a novice's terrors, eyes to mourn his death, beaks to devour him. This unique art's representations blend the contemplative serenity of the statues found in Chartres cathedral and in Egyptian tombs with the artifices of the carnival.

---

*Charles Baudelaire (1821–67) whose celebrated poem *"Correspondances"* inspired the Symbolist movement later in the nineteenth century. The quoted words in this paragraph come from the sonnet's first quatrain, freely translated here.

> La Nature est un temple où de vivants piliers
> Laissent parfois sortir de confuses paroles;
> L'homme y passe à travers des forêts de symboles
> Qui l'observent avec des regards familiers.
>
> [Nature is a temple where living pillars
> Sometimes let out confused words;
> Man journeys through it as if across forests of symbols
> That observe him with friendly eyes.]

The paragraph also alludes in a more general fashion to correspondences, the title of the poem, and to forests of symbols, an image that echoes again in the last sentence of the passage that Lévi-Strauss wrote in 1943 (see p. 8).—Trans.

Vestiges of these two equally great and authentic traditions persist today, preserved in their separate domains, in our cathedrals and our fairgrounds. But here they reign in their primeval unity. This dithyrambic gift for synthesis, this quasi-monstrous ability to perceive the similarity between things which others regard as different, give to the art of British Columbia its unmistakable stamp and genius. From one showcase to the other, from one object to the next, from one corner to another within the same object sometimes, it is as if one were transported from Egypt to twelfth-century France, from the Sassanids to the merry-go-rounds of suburban amusement parks, from the palace of Versailles, with its arrogant emphasis on crests and trophies, its almost shameless recourse to plastic metaphor and allegory, to the forests of the Congo. Look closely at the storage boxes, carved in bas-relief and highlighted in black and red: the ornamentation seems purely decorative. But traditional canons make it possible for a bear, a shark, or a beaver to be reproduced here without any of the constraints that usually bridle the artist. For the animal is represented simultaneously in full face, from the back, and in profile; seen from above and below, from the outside and from within. Using an extraordinary mixture of formalism and realism, a surgeon-draftsman has skinned and boned the animal, removed its entrails, and reconstituted a new creature, all of whose anatomical points coincide with the parallelepiped planes of the box, thus making an object which is simultaneously a box and an animal, and at the same time, one or several animals and a man. The box speaks, it watches efficiently over the treasures that have been entrusted to it in a corner of the house. Furthermore, everything in the house points to the fact that the dwelling is believed to be the carcass of a still larger animal, which one enters through the door, its gaping mouth. In the interior, a forest of symbols, both human and non-human, rise up in a hundred different, sometimes amiable, sometimes tragic, forms."

Wooden storage box, possibly Northern Kwakiutl (British Columbia Provincial Museum, Victoria)

Later I became acquainted with other Northwest Coast collections. Victim, like so many others, of the aberration of curators, the collection at the American Museum of Natural History has lost a good many of the attractions that Franz Boas' method of presentation had managed so well to conserve. Max Ernst, André Breton, Georges Duthuit, and I did gather more modest collections, sharing among ourselves, according to the funds available, the pieces for sale at New York antique dealers. It was a time when these works did not arouse any interest, which, in itself, seems like a myth today. In 1951, I had to sell my collection. Around 1947, when I was cultural counselor at the Embassy, I had had the opportunity of acquiring for France a famous collection, which is now in a museum on the West Coast of the United States; in payment, the seller wanted a few Matisse and Picasso canvasses instead of taxable dollars. But despite all my efforts, I failed to convince the officials responsible for our artistic policy who happened to be visiting New York. True, the national collections did not at that time have modern paintings to spare, and they deemed unrealistic my plan of soliciting the two above-mentioned artists directly. Even though it may have meant granting them a life interest in or ownership of these marvelous objects, once in France, they would surely, sooner or later, have found their way into our museums.

Despite these disappointments, and no doubt partly because of them, there has never been a slackening of the almost carnal bond that has tied me to the art of the Northwest Coast ever since the inter-war period when I first caught sight of the rare specimens to be found in French collections and at a few antique dealers. This sentiment was renewed quite recently near the site where this art was born and developed when I visited the Vancouver and Victoria museums and watched it being revived under the chisel or burin of skillful Indian sculptors, gold- and silversmiths, some of whom are worthy of their great predecessors.

Yet, through the years, my sentiment of profound respect was undermined by a lingering uneasiness: this art posed a problem to me which I could not resolve. Certain masks, all of the same type, were disturbing because of the way they were made. Their style, their shape were strange; their plastic justification escaped me. They were deeply carved by the sculptor's chisel and fitted with appendages, but despite these protruding parts, they presented a massive appearance: they were made to be worn in front of the face, yet they had only slightly concave backs that did not really follow the relief.

Much bigger than life-size, these masks are round at the top, but their sides, which curve inward at first, are then drawn to-

Kwakiutl Xwéxwé mask (courtesy of Museum of the American Indian, Heye Foundation)

gether, becoming parallel or even oblique; the remaining third of the mask thus takes on the rough shape of a rectangle, or an upside-down trapezium. At the lowest extremity, the small base is perfectly horizontal, as if the design had been sawn off in mid-course, representing a sagging lower jaw in the middle of which hangs a large tongue, which is either carved in bas-relief or painted red. The upper jaw protrudes about one third of the way up the mask. Immediately above this, the nose, which is sometimes in-dicated in rough outline or may even be absent, is most often replaced by a very prominent bird head with half-open or closed beak; two or three additional such heads rise like horns on top of the mask. It is variations in the shape of the nose, the number and position of the horns, which distinguish the various types of masks called Beaver, Sawbill Duck, Raven, Snake, and Spring Salmon in certain groups; and Beaver, Sawbill Duck, Raven, Owl, and Spring Salmon in others. But, whatever the type, the general configuration remains the same, as does that of the eyes, consisting of two wood cylinders, either carved into the mass or added on and made to bulge powerfully out of the orbits.

Looking at these masks, I was ceaselessly asking myself the same questions. Why this unusual shape, so ill-adapted to their function? Of course, I was seeing them incomplete because in the old days they were topped by a crown of swan or golden eagle feathers (the former entirely white, the latter white-tipped) intermingled with some thin reeds adorned with "snowballs" of down that quivered with every movement of the wearer. Furthermore, the lower part of the mask rested on a big collarette made in earlier times of stiff plumes, and more recently, of embroidered cloth. But these trimmings, which may be seen in old photographs, rather accentuate the strangeness of the mask without shedding any light on its mysterious aspects: why the gaping mouth, the flabby lower jaw exhibiting an enormous tongue? Why the bird heads, which have no obvious connection with the rest and are most incongruously placed? Why the protruding eyes, which are the unvarying trait of all the types? Finally, why the quasi-demonic style resembling nothing else in the neighboring cultures, or even in the culture that gave it birth?

I was unable to answer any of these questions until I realized that, as is the case with myths, masks, too, cannot be interpreted in and by themselves as separate objects. Looked upon from the semantic point of view, a myth acquires sense only after it is returned to its transformation set. Similarly, one type of mask, con-

Cowichan Swaihwé mask (from Curtis, The North American Indian, *vol. 9, Historical Photography Collection, University of Washington Libraries)*

sidered only from the plastic point of view, echoes other types whose lines and colors it transforms while it assumes its own individuality. For this individuality to stand out against that of another mask, it is necessary that the same relationship exist between the message that the first mask has to transmit or connote and the message that the other mask must convey within the same culture or in a neighboring culture. From this perspective, therefore, it should be noted that the social or religious functions assigned to the various types of mask, which we contrast in order to compare, have the same transformational relationship with each other as exists between the shaping, drawing, and coloring of the masks themselves when we look at them as material objects. Each type of mask is linked to myths whose objective is to explain its legendary or supernatural origin and to lay the foundation for its role in ritual, in the economy, and in the society. My hypothesis, then, which extends to works of art (which, however, are more than works of art) a method validated in the study of myths (which are also works of art), will be proven right if, in the last analysis, we can perceive, between the origin myths for each type of mask, transformational relations homologous to those that, from a purely plastic point of view, prevail among the masks themselves.

To fulfill this program, it is important that we study first the type of mask that I have found so puzzling. We must reassemble the data available about it: that is to say, everything known about its aesthetic characteristics, the technique of its fabrication, its intended use, and the results expected from it; and, finally, about the myths accounting for its origin, the way it looks, its conditions of usage. For it is only after this all-inclusive documentation has been gathered that we may be able to compare it with other records.

2

The Salish Swaihwé

The type of mask I have just described is peculiar to a dozen Indian groups, members of the Salish linguistic family. These groups occupied two territories, each one about three hundred kilometers in length: on the mainland, to the north and south of the Fraser estuary; and, across the Georgia Strait, on the eastern part of Vancouver Island. These masks are generally called Swaihwé.* The phonetic transcriptions adopted by various ethnographers to designate them elsewhere are very similar, and it seems unnecessary to enumerate them, except to point out that, in the Puget Sound region where this mask is unknown, an almost identical word, *sqwéqwé,* designates the potlatch, a type of ceremony in the course of which a host distributes riches to guests whom he has assembled to validate, by their presence, his accession to a new title or his passage to a new status. I will come back to this analogy.

The color white was dominant in the costume of the wearers of the mask. The collarette, already mentioned, was made of swan's

---

*The Salish phoneme generally represented by *h* or *x* is an uvular fricative. From the phonetic point of view, a more accurate transcription would be: *sxwaixwe.*

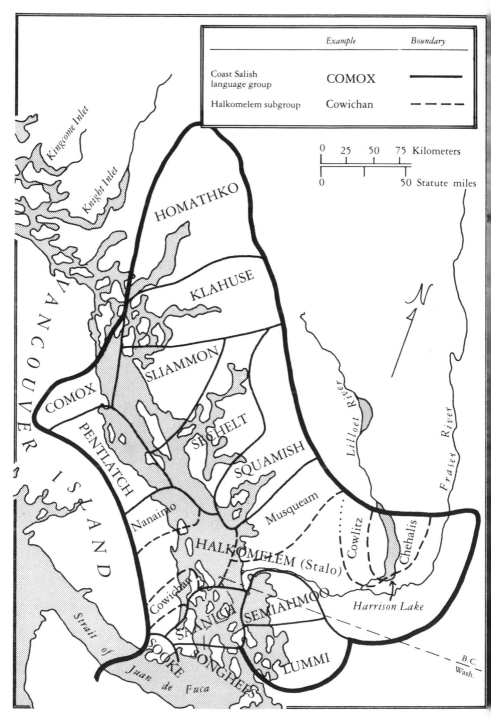

Map 1. *Distribution of the Coast Salish Swaihwé mask*

feathers, as were the skirt, the leggings, and the armlets (sometimes made of loon skin) girdling the dancers. Instead of plumes, certain northern groups, the Klahuse and the Sliammon, used a species of glistening grass, also white. In their hands, the masked dancers held a special sistrum (rattle) made of scallop shells strung on a wooden ring. At the time when Curtis visited the Cowichan of Vancouver Island, there were among these Indians seven owners of the Swaihwé mask who put in an appearance on potlatch occasions but were absent from the winter rites. Whoever wanted to give a potlatch or other profane feast paid the owners of the mask to insure their participation. As they danced, they pointed to the sky, a reminder that, as we shall see, their ancestors had descended from there. The Musqueam of the Fraser estuary, who got the mask from groups upriver, would book it for potlatches, marriages, funerals, and the profane dances that accompanied initiations. In certain estuary groups, a ceremonial clown, wearing a somewhat different mask, would attack the Swaihwé masks with a lance as if to put out the eyes, and the dancers would pretend to chase him.

Pecten shell rattle, carried by Swaihwé dancer (courtesy of Museum of the American Indian, Heye Foundation)

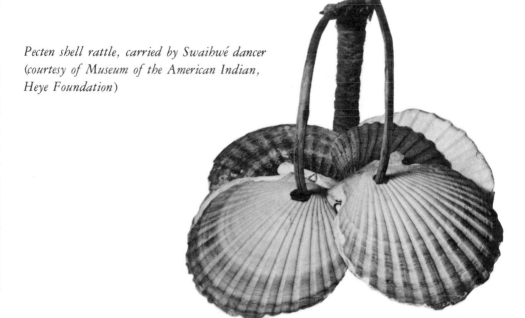

Cowichan Swaihwé dancer holding pecten shell rattle (from Curtis, The North American Indian, *vol. 9, Historical Photography Collection, University of Washington Libraries)*

*Salish (Musqueam) Swaihwé mask
(University of British Columbia
Museum of Anthropology)*

The Swaihwé masks, and the right to wear them in the ceremonies, belonged exclusively to a few lineages of high rank. These
privileges were transmitted through inheritance or marriage: a
woman, member of a mask-owning lineage, passed this right on
to the children she bore her husband. This explains how, from
perhaps a single point of origin, the mask spread from the main-

land to Vancouver Island and over an area of about two hundred kilometers north and south of the Fraser estuary. On the island, among the Cowichan and their Nanaimo neighbors, the bringing out of the masks had a purificatory role: it "washed" the spectators. And, throughout the area under consideration, the masks brought luck and facilitated the acquisition of wealth.

Although this latter function is present everywhere, and one may therefore see in it an invariant attribute of the masks, the myths relating to their origin differ distinctly according to whether the masks come from the island or from the mainland coast.

The island versions relate that, in earliest times, when the ancestors of the masks dropped from the sky, their faces were in every detail like the present masks. Two personages first arrived on earth; they chased away the third who was following close on their heels, lest his body odor, say some, the noise of his rattle, say others, scare away the salmon. Upon touching the ground, the fourth one caused an earthquake. They were six in all and each one brought along a particular good: weapon, hunting or fishing trap, domestic utensil, magical remedy, and so on.

A man was living in the region already. He had a daughter, and, as she was lazy, he married her off to one of the newcomers who was reputed to be a good huntsman. Accompanied by two slaves, the young girl traveled over a long road to reach her intended to whom she offered dried salmon. The travelers received meat in exchange. But the marriage turned out badly. The three children to whom the wife gave birth died in infancy, and her husband sent her back to her father.

The same ancestor then decided to marry the daughter whom one of his companions had had with a wife from another country. They had many children. One day, in the company of his brother (who had arrived from the sky immediately after him), he discovered the dog who now helped them in the hunt. But despite his older brother's warnings, the younger ancestor became guilty of sexual incontinence with his own wife: as predicted, the dog disappeared. The two men left in search of it and arrived at a waterfall over which the salmon were attempting to swim. They pondered about this; they made basket-traps and suspended them all along the falls; many of the leaping fish tumbled into the nets. The brothers dried the fish in quantity and, loaded with their provisions, returned to the village.

Although more fully developed than others which I need not go into, this version, nevertheless, still lacks coherence. The episodes are unconnected, and the story ends abruptly with a fishing trip that has no role in the plot and does not bring it to conclusion. Yet, one discerns several parallels: the principal ancestor contracts two successive marriages, one with a spouse who is both *anterior* (she was on earth before him) and *distant* since she belonged to a different people; and the other with a spouse who is both *posterior* (born well after his arrival on earth) and *proximate* (daughter of one of his companions).

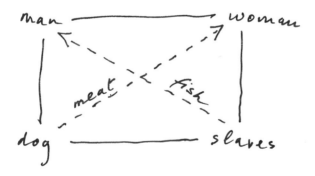

In the course of each marriage, two types of auxiliaries manifest themselves: the first wife's slaves, who are fishermen and probably male, and the hunting dog, which is discovered soon after the second marriage. As a matter of fact, in Salish thought, the dog is a kind of slave: "Even a dog or a slave will do his best if you treat him well," as the saying goes around Puget Sound. We do not know if the mythic animal is male or female, but the inland Salish made a connection between women and dogs. An Okanogan myth explains "why we have women and dogs now." While ritually invoking the soul of a bear killed in the hunt, a hunter promises him, "no woman shall eat your flesh; no dogs shall insult you." Women and dogs were not allowed to urinate near the men's sweathouses, and any dog caught urinating in the same place as a woman was killed. In the houses of the Carrier (who are Athapaskan neighbors of the Salish), the area near the doorway was assigned to women and dogs. In fact, in the myth I have just related, the strengthening of the bond between the hunter and his dog depends on a slackening of that between him and his spouse. By showing too much passion, the husband hurts his wife because this violation of hunting taboos deprives him of his dog's services and he cannot, therefore, kill the game which it is a husband's duty to supply to his spouse. To this double fault of a husband toward his wife correspond, in the first part of the myth, a woman's faults toward her father and her husband: fault against culture when the lazy miss refuses to sew skins to make clothes, and fault against nature when, once married, she proves unable to beget viable children. As far as everything else in the myth is concerned, the island versions remain impervious to all efforts at formalization. Only when they are compared with the mainland versions can their construction be clearly seen. Let me consider those now.

With minor differences, all the groups of the middle and lower Fraser tell the same story. There was once a young boy who was afflicted with a kind of leprosy. His body gave out a stinking smell, and even his close relatives ran away from him. The poor fellow decided to commit suicide by throwing himself into a lake. He sank to the bottom of the water, onto the roof of a house guarded by loons (*Gavia* sp.) and whose every inhabitant suffered from a mysterious ailment (or, according to some versions, only a baby or the chief's daughter was sick; they had convulsions whenever the hero spat on their back or stomach). In exchange for his own cure, he in turn cured the one (or many) sick, won the young girl's hand in marriage, and saw the Swaihwé dancers' masks, rattles, and costumes for the first time. Following this, he found himself miraculously transferred back to the spot from which he had plunged; or else, the beaver and the coho salmon (and sometimes more numerous animals; see names given to the masks, p. 12, above) opened up an underground passage for him that led to a site near the present town of Yale.

The hero sent or led his sister to the lake and ordered her to cast her fishing line into it, with or without hook (with feathers as bait in one version). She caught and brought to the surface the Water People. The latter freed themselves and went back to the deep, leaving behind a mask and a rattle. The two youngsters placed these precious objects in a decorated basket, especially braided for the occasion, or they enveloped them in the most beautiful blanket owned by their mother. Sometimes the hero returns the original mask to the water after having made a copy of it, which he entrusts to his cousin to wear in public (because, says the myth, he does not himself have the means to show it); sometimes, for the same reason, he gives the original to his brother. But whether the original or a copy is involved, in nearly all the versions, the mask is passed on as dowry to the hero's sister or daughter when she marries. Only one version deviates from the norm when it relates that the mask fell into the hands of enemies. For it was precious indeed: on its first owner it conferred the power to cure convulsions and skin diseases, and, generally, says the same version of the myth, "everything seems to come easy to those who have the mask."

The mainland myths offer another common trait: they give a definite geographical location for their plot. It is, say some, Iwawus or Ewawus, a village about three kilometers upriver from present-day Hope. The lake where the hero seeks his death is Lake Kaukwe, or Kawkawa, near the mouth of the river Coquihalla, a left-bank tributary of the Fraser, which it meets at the level of Hope. After an underground journey, the hero emerges near Yale, and it is toward Yale also that his family goes fishing.

The Thompson Indians of the Utamqt group have a version which is very close to the preceding ones. They call the village Wa'us and situate it four or five kilometers east of Hope. This version poses a problem to which chapter 12 in Part II is especially devoted. A version originating from the lower Fraser gives more importance to the sister. In the beginning of the story, she lives alone with her brother. When she brings up the mask that the people of the lake have fastened to her hook, she thinks, at first, that she has caught a fish; she gets a fright when she sees the feathers and runs away. Her brother sends her back, she starts all over again, grasps the mask at last, wraps it in a blanket, and puts it in her basket. Her brother displays it in certain dances. Henceforth, the mask will be passed on through inheritance or marriage, but it may also be stolen during wars, an accident of little consequence since outsiders do not know the songs and dances that make the mask effective.

At the mouth of Harrison River, and also on the lower Fraser, it is said that the first ancestor had two sons and two daughters. The latter went fishing every morning. One day they brought up something heavy at the end of their line and saw the protruding eyes and the feathers of the Swaihwé (Sqoâéqoé). They called their father; the supernatural being disappeared, abandoning its mask and its dress. The descendants of this family took wives in foreign tribes and that is how the wearing of the mask spread.

In July 1974, I heard a slightly different version originating from Sardis, near Chilliwack on the lower Fraser. According to this myth, the mask was fished out of Harrison Lake by two un-married sisters who were fiercely opposed to marriage, a feeling shared by their brother. The mask had a long beak and was adorned with feathers, which one day saved the brother when he was being pursued by enemies: he escaped by swimming unsuspected under the feathers, which alone were visible on the surface of the water. This incident showed the virtues of the mask. Later, a shaman made it complete with a dancing dress made of eagle plumes. The two sisters relented and consented to get married, one into the Squamish, the other into the Sumas tribe.

As do some other versions that I will examine, this one implicitly evokes a quasi-incestuous initial situation: the brother and sisters are unnaturally drawn together by their common hostility to marriage, which incites them to live together; but in the end, and as usual, the acquisition of the mask and its usage lead the women to exogamous marriages. As for the theme of the floating lure, it recalls a similar episode in the Squamish version (see p. 32), which originates precisely from one of the two groups into which the two heroines marry.*

South of the United States–Canadian border, the Lummi of Washington State give the Sxoaxi mask a somewhat different shape: a big face whose mouth misses one or two front teeth, allowing the wearer to peep through the interstice. A raven's head with beak pointed downward takes the place of the nose; toward the top, the face continues with a human form whose round head surmounts the mask that bristles with fine twigs on which tufts of swan's down have been glued. The dancer, naked to the waist, wore a skirt made of wild goat's hair and leggings of swan's skin, and held in his hand a rattle of the type already described (see p. 17). It was believed that any person who usurped the mask would get sores all over his face. A comedian took part in the dances. He wore a mask, which was red on one side and black on the

---

*I thank Chief Malloway of Sardis, who kindly told me this tale, and also Drs. W. G. Jilek and L. M. Jilek-Aall who arranged the meeting with him.

other, with a twisted mouth and disorderly hair. The spectators were not supposed to laugh at the sight of him, or else they too would become afflicted with sores on the body and the respiratory tract. This comedian annoyed the masked dancers by all sorts of antics and, in particular, picked at their eyes, which, as usual, were strongly protruding.

The Sxoaxi masks appeared in profane ceremonies such as potlatches. Dancers who had earned the protection of a guardian spirit were excluded from taking part for fear that the spirit might spoil the character of the ceremony by manifesting itself inappropriately. The myth of origin deserves special attention. Here it is.

A motherless boy was undergoing training for initiation. His father treated him harshly, inflicting all sorts of tests upon him, even forbidding him to associate with his only sister. The latter took pity and went to see him in secret; she promised her brother that she would accompany him on his next errand to help him find a little food. She gave him fern roots, but, on the way back, the boy was very sick; at once suspecting some disobedience, the father threw him out and presaged an early death for him.

The hero ventured off on his own and sores broke out all over his body. Certain that he was about to die, he resolved to walk such a long distance that his remains would not be found. One day, exhausted by fatigue and illness, he stopped near a stream. Two painted men, one red, the other black, came to him in a dream and predicted that the next day he would find two salmon, one red, one black. He should prepare them according to ritual, cook them, and place them on a bed of skunk cabbage (*Lysichitum*), but, no matter how much he craved them, he must abstain from eating them. If he did this, he would no longer suffer from hunger. This bicolored pair of salmon challenging the hero obviously recalls the dancer bedecked with a half-red–half-black mask who, in his own way, taunts the wearers of the Sxoaxi masks. The exploration of this trail cannot go further for lack of information. Let me therefore return to the myth.

The hero followed the prescriptions of his nocturnal visitors to the letter: frogs came out of his cheeks and chest and leaped onto the salmon. The next night, the two men reappeared; they ordered their protégé to follow the course of a torrent that penetrated deep into the mountains. He let himself be carried by the current to a vast dwelling on whose walls dance costumes were hung. An old man received him, excused himself for not being able to give him anything on the spot: "Go back to your village," he said, "ask them to clean up your house and tell them to have two baskets made for you." His host went on to say that on the following day the hero's sister should cut three strands of hair and, after splicing them end to end, she should cast them into the water like a fishing line.

The sister did as he bade her and drew up the line when she felt it heavy. Rumblings were heard coming from the bottom of the water. The young girl pulled up to the bank a mask which she thought hideous and to which were attached two rattles. She then fished out a second mask; her brother put each one in a basket. When night came, in front of the assembled village he intoned the song of the masks, which he made some robust young men, chosen from among his near relations, wear. Eventually, different villages engaged him to show the masks at their ceremonials, and he became very rich.

It will be seen that, in contrast to their island counterparts, the mainland versions have a clear and well-constructed plot. But it is also evident that the seeming incoherence of the former is due to the fact that they simply reverse all the episodes. Thus, they have to work out a different plot that will allow a restringing of the segments, even though it means changing the sequence and plac-

A Swaihwé dance, photographed at the beginning of the twentieth century

(*British Columbia Provincial Museum, Victoria*)

ing at the end of the tale the transformed image of an episode which in the original is found at the beginning.

Indeed, this manipulation shows through in the first origin attributed to the masks here and there. In the Fraser version, they must be hoisted laboriously from their underwater abode up to the surface of the earth; in the island version, they drop spontaneously from the sky without external intervention. Although the landing site, that is, the ground, remains the same, in one case they come from the sky, thus from above; in the other case they come from the chthonian world, which the myths situate at the bottom of the waters. In all their details, the island and mainland coast versions maintain among themselves this same relationship of inversion. The former keep the link between the husband and wife in the forefront of the intrigue, the latter underscore that between brother and sister. The initial episode of the coastal myth has a mother's son (one version specifies that the father is dead), diseased and incurable, who is kept at a distance because of his stench and who throws himself into the water (thus going in an up–down direction along a vertical axis). The island version responds to this with, on the one hand, a father's daughter (the myths say nothing about the maternal parent), lazy and incompetent, who travels far to find a husband (along a horizontal axis); and, on the other hand, the third ancestor who has fallen from the sky and is kept at a distance for fear that the noise of his rattle or his body odor might frighten off the fish. Only the Lummi version adopts the father–son formula, specifying that the mother is dead, but at the cost of an inversion that opposes this mainland variant to all the others. For in it, the hero falls ill *as a result of* his disobedience, and the disobedience is the reason for the exile he endures, while in other versions he goes into voluntary exile *because of* his illness.

In the island versions, the lazy young girl marries the first mask; but, since all children born of their union die in infancy, she deprives the mask of the means of becoming an ancestor. In the mainland versions, on the contrary, the diseased young man marries the daughter of the chief of the Water People, who is the first of the masks, and he also cures all the others, who, thanks to his marriage and to their recovery, will now be able to become ancestors. Later, the heroine of the island versions and the hero of the mainland one are returned, she to her father, he to his mother. The first mask of the island versions then marries a close relative who is not a sister, while in the myths of the mainland, the hero enlists his sister to whom, in the Lummi version especially, he is united by an almost incestuous intimacy. This excessive intimacy echoes the sexual incontinence of which, in the island versions, one of the protagonists is guilty with his wife, and this in spite of the fact that the two types of closeness had been prohibited, by the hero's father in one case and by the brother of the individual in question in the other case.

Now we understand the purpose of the bizarre fishing trip with which the island versions abruptly end. Having placed the masks' origin at the beginning instead of at the end of the tale, and having the masks fall from the sky—in contrast with the mainland versions where they are pulled up from the bottom of the water— the island versions literally do not know how to finish the story. They need a conclusion—but, of necessity, the conclusion of the mainland versions can only survive in the paradoxical form of the out-of-water catch of fishes that strive to run up a fall and drop back into basketry nets. This arrangement of the myth exactly counterbalances the fishing of masks from the bottom of the water and the placing of them in specially made baskets. Thus we obtain two symmetrical conclusions: one where humans use a line to fish masks out of the water, and then put them in baskets; the other where supernatural beings, who are the prototypes of the masks, manufacture baskets which they hang in the open air. They use a technique especially invented to catch fish that are transported out of the water by an acrobatic feat.

I draw two conclusions from this analysis. One notices first that it is easier to transform the mainland versions into the island ones than it is to carry out this operation in reverse. For the mainland versions are built logically, whereas the island ones are not; the latter acquire a logic derived from the former if, and only if, we see the island versions as the result of a transformation whose initial state is illustrated by the mainland versions. It follows from this that the mainland versions must be deemed original, and those from the island derivative, thus confirming the opinion of specialists in this region of the world who place the origin and center of diffusion of the Swaihwé masks in the middle Fraser. They use rather vague arguments, however, which are less convincing than those drawn from the comparison I have just elaborated. Thus, far from turning its back on history, structural analysis makes a contribution to it.

This being the case, I note the hybrid character of a Squamish version, which seems to have as its principal aim to explain an ancient migration from the coast to the island.

In the beginning, when there were still very few people on earth, two brothers heard a noise on the roof of their house. It was a man dancing, wearing a Sxaixi (Swaihwé) mask. They invited him to come down, but the man refused and continued to dance. Finally, he agreed but announced forthwith that he was their eldest brother. "No," said the brothers, "we are the elder ones, you have just arrived, you are the youngest." Whereupon, the man resumed his non-stop dancing. Exasperated, the brothers drove him out downriver all the way to a bay. There the stranger married a woman of unknown origin; they had numerous descendants who were endowed with a lively and energetic temperament. Sometimes sea lions would visit a reef near their village. When they heard the animals bellow, the inhabitants of the original upriver settlement, which was more distant from the shore, rushed to the bay; but it was all wasted effort—their rivals, being on the spot, had already killed everything. This state of affairs went from bad to worse till famine reigned among the first inhabitants.

They had a sorcerer among them who thought up a stratagem. He spent months, perhaps years, manufacturing a replica of a sea lion. When it appeared on the river, the people upriver pretended to start hunting. The people downriver, alerted by the commotion, wanted to be the first to harpoon the false game, which lured them further upriver. Then it went down the river again, carrying along the men who were hooked to the harpoon rope and, in their trail, the women and children who had packed and boarded canoes. The wooden sea lion headed for the big island. Some families, whose men had let go of the rope in mid-course, landed on Kuper Island (very near Vancouver Island, facing the Fraser estuary). Those who held fast arrived at Nanoose (a little farther to the north, on the coast of Vancouver Island). That is why the Squamish of the mainland coast are friends of the people who live on the other side of the strait.

This version confirms my interpretation, because as the story unfolds between the mainland and the island, it always adopts intermediate courses. Instead of falling from the sky or surfacing from the bottom of the lake, the first mask suddenly appears on the roof of a house: halfway between up-above and down-below, on the same spot where in the "water" versions the hero lands when he pays an involuntary visit to the people of the lake (see p. 22). He is greeted by two brothers, an unmarked pair in whom the marked opposition of a husband and wife or of a brother and sister is neutralized. Although still of relatively celestial origin, this mask is not the first ancestor, since the brothers and their fellow men were already inhabiting the earth. These characters play a more important role than the very unobtrusive one assigned to the single individual recognized as the first occupant of earth by the island versions. Finally, the opposition between the horizontal and vertical axes is neutralized as well, since the mask comes down only from the roof of a house; and the sea lion hunt, which takes place entirely on the surface of the water, replaces line fishing from the chthonian abysses.

Let me now come to the second point. We have seen that in passing from the mainland versions to the island ones, the final episode substitutes fish for masks. The masks were surely fish already in the mainland version, not literally, granted, but in the figurative sense, since they are fished with a line. And, is it not because they are compared with fish, in the literal and figurative senses, that they have a strikingly dangling tongue? A Coeur d'Alene myth (thus also Salish, but from the interior) tells of a water spirit caught by a woman who took its tongue for a fish. Reversing this analogy—and the comparison of more or less distant myths often confirms this kind of transformation—the Clackamas Chinook of the lower Columbia know of an ogre named "Tongue" after its voracious tongue of fire, which gets sliced up by fish with sharp spiny fins. These fish must be Scorpaenidae, which we shall meet again later. From the Salish of Vancouver Island comes a sculpture representing a Swaihwé mask, with the effigy of a fish set out in relief in the place usually occupied by the tongue; on the other hand, inland, from the Lilloet to the Shuswap, there is a prevailing belief in half-human–half-fish Water People (or Mermen). All these facts suggest a double affinity between the Swaihwé masks and fish: a metaphorical affinity, since the large lolling tongue, which is one of their distinguishing characteristics, looks like a fish and may be mistaken for one; and a metonymical affinity insofar as they are fished and it is by the tongue that fish are caught. "The water monster woman," goes another Coeur d'Alene myth, "sat there with the hook in her mouth. . . ."

Among other interior Salish, I have just mentioned the Lilloet. It cannot be said categorically that their Säinnux masks corresponded to the Swaihwé masks of their Fraser neighbors, since no specimen is known to have survived to the present. This seems probable, however, if we consider, on the one hand, the carved poles found in Lilloet territory, on which Swaihwé masks can easily be recognized; and, on the other hand, the fact that, like the Swaihwé masks, those called Säinnux were the privilege of particular lineages who wore them on potlatch occasions, and that they represented beings which were half-men—half-fish. I will return to this point in Part II. The myth of origin is different, however, despite certain analogies: a visit to supernatural beings, dwelling underground, who are friends of the water and powerful magicians. But, instead of the hero, who visits them involuntarily, making them sick, then curing them and receiving a spouse in gratitude, in this case it is the Water People who cause the death of the young men who come in the hope of marrying their daughters. One of the young men, endowed with magical powers, finally succeeds in befriending his hosts and seducing two sisters because of his luminous body, which is smooth to the touch. He is thus the opposite of a leper, though he later transforms himself into an invalid old man whom one of his wives (the only one who would not desert him) carries around in a basket.

Other aspects of the origin myths of the Swaihwé masks are met again among the Lilloet, but in connection with the origin of copper. It is known that the peoples of this part of the world valued this metal highly. In early times, they obtained it through barter with northern tribes who, in their turn, procured it from Indians of the Athapaskan linguistic family who extracted it in its native state. In historical times, navigators and traders introduced sheet copper, which quickly replaced the other kind.

A grandmother and her grandson, say the Lilloet, were the only survivors of an epidemic. As the child cried constantly, to amuse him, the old woman made a fishing line with her hair and put a ball of hair on the hook as bait. Thus equipped, the young hero caught the first copper, the talisman that made him a good hunter.

His grandmother dried the meat, tanned and sewed the skins; they became rich. The hero decided to travel. He made the acquaintance of the Squamish and invited them as well as other tribes to various feasts. In front of his guests, he sang, danced, exhibited his copper, and distributed the accumulated riches. Two chiefs offered him their daughters in marriage: in exchange, they received pieces of copper. The young man and his wives had many children, especially sons, to whom other chiefs gave their daughters, receiving copper in their turn. That is how the metal spread to all the tribes. Those who possessed it regarded it as a very precious good with which they did not want to part, such high standing did this rare material bestow on them.

This myth, then, attributes to copper the same aquatic origin as the other myths lend to the Swaihwé mask. The one is fished for like the other, and, similarly, their ownership procures wealth. Furthermore, copper and mask spread by way of marriages contracted with alien groups, with this difference, that the direction of the circulation is not the same: the Swaihwé mask goes from the wife to the husband and their descendants, while the copper goes from the husband to the wife's father, thus to an ascendant. It seems as if, by passing from the tribes of the Fraser to the Lilloet, the Swaihwé origin myth undergoes a kind of fission. It is met again, in part, in the origin myth of the Säinnux masks (which are probably the same as the Swaihwé); and, in part, in copper's origin myth. The copper is a metallic substance without obvious relation to the masks, although from an economic and sociological angle it fulfills the same function, with the proviso that the direction in which the gifts circulate is reversed.

A Skagit myth tells the same story as the Fraser myths about the Swaihwé, except that the supernatural beings who live at the bottom of the waters grant their visitor, not masks but "all the property and goods" of the four cardinal points: goods comparable to those procured elsewhere, by either the mask or the copper. At

Kwakiutl copper (University of British Columbia Museum of Anthropology)

the other extremity of the Swaihwé masks' area of diffusion, the
Kwakiutl have a myth about a boy called He'kîn. Always ill, his
skin covered with sores, he seeks refuge at the summit of a mountain to await death. A she-toad on the spot cures him with a
magic medicine, gives him a decorated copper sheet (those strange
objects which the Kwakiutl and their neighbors considered their
most precious possessions and which played a considerable role in
social, economic, and ritual transactions), and she confers on him

the name of Copper-Maker, Laqwagila. The hero returns to his family. His sister greets him and congratulates him on his new appearance. He gives her the copper as a present "so that she may carry it in dowry to her future husband."

Despite its inversion of the site where the hero seeks death (the top of a mountain instead of a deep lake), this myth assigns to the origin of the copper the same intrigue and several of the details which struck us as significant in the origin myths of the Swaihwé, in particular the role given to the sister. Even the helpful she-toad was already present in these myths, in the shape of frogs, which, in the Lummi version, escape from the hero's body and rid him of his illness. This batrachian also plays a part in a version from the lower Fraser already used (see p. 22), although I did not mention this episode: when the hero stops on the shore of the lake where he wants to drown himself, he first catches a salmon and roasts it; but as he is about to eat it, he finds a frog in its place. This blow of fate taxes him to the limit and he puts his project into execution. As it is necessary for him to throw himself into the water to meet the healing spirits (givers of the masks), it can be said that the frog, substituting itself for the salmon, is the indirect cause of his good fortune. Similarly, in the Lummi version, the frogs rid him of their malevolent presence in exchange, it could be said, for his renunciation of the two salmon on which the batrachians leap, as if to merge with or to replace them (see p. 27). Both the Kwakiutl and the Salish myths put the she-toad in correlation with and opposition to the salmon, and they give the batrachian an identical role, in a plot involving the acquisition of either the copper or the Swaihwé.

A few provisional conclusions emerge from all that has preceded. I have shown certain invariant traits of the Swaihwé masks seen from their plastic aspect, as well as from the point of view of their origin myths. These plastic invariants include the white color of the costume, due to the frequent use of swan's feathers and of down; the lolling tongue and the protuberant eyes of the masks; and, finally, the bird heads, which sometimes replace the nose or surmount the head. Assuming next the sociological point of view, we note that possession of or assistance from the mask favored the acquisition of wealth; that masks appeared in potlatches and other profane ceremonies, but were excluded from the sacred winter rites; that, properly speaking, they belonged to a few noble lineages and were passed on solely through inheritance and marriage. Finally, from the semantic point of view, the myths bring out a double affinity in the Swaihwé masks: on the one hand with fish, and on the other with copper. Is it possible to understand the reason for these scattered traits and to articulate them into a system? At the point we have reached, this is the dual problem posed by the Swaihwé masks.

3

The Kwakiutl Xwéxwé

On Vancouver Island, Salish language groups were neighbors of the Nootka to the west and of the Kwakiutl to the north. This proximity explains how these two peoples came to borrow the Swaihwé masks from the Salish, including even their name, which in Kwakiutl is pronounced Xwéxwé or Kwékwé. More realistic in their manufacture, the Nootka and Kwakiutl masks represent a strongly expressive face, while preserving all the characteristics that I have distinguished in the Swaihwé. They are adorned with wild goose down. Certain specimens of Kwakiutl origin are painted white and bear, on the upper part, stylized motifs reminiscent of the feathers that decorate the same masks among the Salish. And all the Xwéxwé masks, Nootka as well as Kwakiutl, have the lolling tongue, the bulging eyes, and the appendages in the shape of bird heads—these last sometimes whimsically distributed. The dancers carried a sistrum identical to that of the Swaihwé. It is undoubtedly the same mask, transposed into a style that is less hieratic, more lyrical, and more violent.

The Kwakiutl linked the Xwéxwé masks with earthquakes. Their dance, wrote Boas, "is believed to shake the ground and to be a certain means of bringing back the hamatsa," that is, the new initiate to the highest ranking secret society, the Cannibals. Dur-

Nootka Xwéxwé mask (University of British Columbia Museum of Anthro-pology)

ing initiation, the novice became ferocious and wild and ran in the woods: the objective was to bring him back to reintegrate him in the village community. This association of the Xwéxwé (or Swaihwé) with earthquakes was already in evidence in the Salish myths (pp. 20, 27) and it throws a curious light on the symbolism of the sistrums carried by the dancers, as it does also on that of the quivering twigs tipped with "snowballs" of down, which adorn the top of the Salish masks. In *From Honey to Ashes,* I drew atten-

Kwakiutl ceremonial rattle representing a severed head, used to pacify the Cannibal dancer (British Columbia Provincial Museum, Victoria)

tion to the way Plutarch explained the role of sistrums among the ancient Egyptians: "The sistrum . . . makes it clear that all things in existence need to be shaken, or rattled about, and never to cease from motion but, as it were, to be waked up and agitated when they grow drowsy and torpid." The sistrum was a symbol of the god with the welded thighs who "for shame tarried in the wilderness; but Isis, by severing and separating those parts of his body, provided him with means of rapid progress." One is reminded of the hero whom disease had rendered infirm in the Swaihwé origin myths, and also, as I emphasized in my earlier work, of the Karaja Indians' demiurge whose arms and legs were tied to prevent him from destroying the earth by floods and other disasters. According to Dr. Gloria Cranmer Webster, curator at the Museum of Anthropology in Vancouver at that time and Kwakiutl by birth; the Xwéxwé masks did not want to stop dancing once they got started; they had to be physically constrained to do so. Also, they would prevent the children from laying hands on presents (in recent times, coins), which were randomly thrown at them during the spectacle. I will return to this detail, which is all the more interesting since at the other extremity of the Swaihwé diffusion area, the Lummi chose the strongest men to wear the masks in the hope that they would dance a very long time. These athletes eventually would give way to the person in whose honor the feast was being held, and it was this person who distributed gifts all around, under the watchful eye of the youngest spectators, who were on the lookout for the opportunity of a scramble to seize them.

To account for the origin of the masks, the Kwakiutl had two types of stories; some frankly mythic, others of rather legendary character. Roughly true to historical fact, these latter tales refer to marriages concluded with the Comox, a Salish people who are neighbors of the Southern Kwakiutl on Vancouver Island. One of

them begins at the moment when a chief of the Fort Rupert region—the territory of the Kwagiutl subgroup—had his herald an-
nounce that he wants to marry the daughter of the Comox chief.
Immediately following this proclamation, he set off to sea with a
large crew. The Comox gave them a good welcome and accepted
the wedding presents, which filled two vessels, and the bride-to-
be packed her baggage. A thundering noise was then heard while
shell-rattles kept jingling: four masked personages appeared and
began to dance. In the course of the banquet that followed, the
Kwakiutl tasted the camas (Liliaceae, with edible bulbs) for the
first time. The Comox chief ordered that the masks be "pacified,"
then handed them over to his son-in-law as gifts. In addition, the
son-in-law received a new name and twenty cases of camas to
which, upon his return home, he treated his people. He then ordered the Swaihwé to dance. His wife gave him three children,
but, after the birth of the fourth, the couple separated; the wife
returned to her native village with two of the children and the
right, for the Comox, to perform a few Kwakiutl dances of the
winter rite. The two children had Kwakiutl names, which, through
them, went for the first time to the Comox.

Another legendary tale concerns two Comox who went to the
Kwakiutl hoping to find a wife for their grandson and son. The
suitor was approved, received a new name (that of the young girl's
paternal grandfather), gave a potlatch to his new relations, and
got as a gift the mask of Sisiutl, the double-headed serpent, whose
dance he was thus able to perform in front of his Comox family
who had never seen it. He established himself among the Kwakiutl, but his father took charge of returning the Sisiutl to the
Comox. It is since that time that these Indians have celebrated the
winter rite, of which the Sisiutl dance is a part.

Kwakiutl Xwéxwé mask (British Columbia Provincial Museum, Victoria)

Kwakiutl ceremonial curtain representing Sisiutl below, with copper, rainbow, and ravens above (University of British Columbia Museum of Anthropology)

A third story features, apart from the Comox, two Kwakiutl groups related by marriage: the island Nimkish and, just across from them on the mainland, the Koeksotenok. The Nimkish chief lived in Xulk, on the east coast of the island. One day, he started a discussion with his son-in-law on the "good dance" of the Comox, that is, the Swaihwé. This son-in-law had a brother whom he persuaded to wage war against the Comox in order to take possession of the dance. The young man embarked with one hundred vigorous warriors. When they arrived in sight of the Comox country, they heard the sound of thunder: it was the strangers who "were singing for the Xwéxwé." The troop disembarked at the other extremity of the bay, from which could be seen the dancers and clouds of eagle's down rising as high as the sky. After the dance, half of the ship's crew approached and the Comox sat them down and treated them to a feast. Again there was a roar of thunder and four masked dancers appeared, painted with ochre, covered with feathers, and in their hands holding rattles made of threaded scallop shells. The Comox chief harangued his visitors and granted them the right to perform the dance, and he also gave them a chest containing the masks with their accessories.

Between the island Salish and the Kwakiutl (of both the island and the mainland) there existed, therefore, a network of ambiguous relationships which could include everything from matrimonial alliance to war. In both cases, the masks and the privileges attached to them were the objects of rivalries and trade, on the same basis as women, proper names, and foodstuffs. The Swaihwé or Xwéxwé mask in these tales, being excluded from the sacred winter rites, passes from the Salish to the Kwakiutl on the occasion of a warring expedition or a marriage; in this latter case, the transfer is made in the same direction as that of the bride. By contrast, as an integral part of the winter rites, the Sisiutl mask goes in the reverse direction, from the Kwakiutl to the Comox, which is also what the young Comox bridegroom does when he settles down with his in-laws. Such stories undoubtedly originate from customs which once existed. Others obviously pertain to mythology.

For instance, the story of this Kwakiutl Indian of the Nimkish group, who wanted to go from the town of Xulk (already mentioned) where he lived, to the head of Cape Scott, at the northern extremity of the island, to visit a place made famous by a mythical event.* In the evening, he arrived at Gwegwakawalis, a small bay

---

*Two eagles and their young one day descended from the sky. They alighted at Qum'qate, near Cape Scott, took off their bird skins and became humans, the first people of the region. If this is the event referred to here, it is significant that it preserves the code of the island Salish Swaihwé origin myths, whose message alone survives, inverted, in the present myth, which transposes it into the terms of a code that is no longer celestial, but aquatic.

at the foot of the cape, built a small house for himself, lit a fire, dined, but could not sleep. During the night he heard a rumble, and the ground shook as if in an earthquake. He came out, sat down, and overheard a murmur of conversation that seemed to originate from Axdem, on the opposite side of the cape. He went back to bed and fell asleep. A man came to him in a dream and ordered him to purify himself, to go to Axdem and, once there, after four earth tremors, to enter a ceremonial house which he would see, to sit down there and wait. The same vision appeared to him the following night. During these two days, the hero bathed, fasted, then took the road to Axdem.

He arrived there at nightfall, saw a big house and went in. A fire lit itself spontaneously in the middle; soon, a troop of men and women appeared, and an orator addressed an invocation to the spirits. Four times, the women changed themselves into big red codfishes, animated by convulsive movements, which were the cause of the rumblings heard by the hero; after the convulsions, they reassumed their human shape. Four characters wearing Xwéxwé masks danced in front of them jangling the shell rattles. In the meantime, those officiating sang:

> Go away, ugly ones (*twice*)
> Ugly ones with lolling tongues (*twice*)
> Ugly ones with protruding eyes (*twice*)

Each time the dancers exited, the fishes changed back into women.

The orator greeted the hero, conferred upon him the name Red Codfish, and presented him with "the supernatural treasures of this great ceremonial." The hero asked that the ceremonial house be delivered to his home. He was told to go back to his place and that the house and accessories would follow. Our man therefore returned to Xulk, stayed in bed four days, then summoned the whole population whom he entreated to wash before the meeting. In the evening, the whisperings of invisible beings told him that his ceremonial house had arrived. He entered it with his guests. Rumblings were heard, the earth shook four times, the masks appeared and danced. The hero showed everyone the gifts he had received from the fishes: the four sculptured posts of the house, the four Xwéxwé masks, the four wooden drums and notched sticks, which, when sawed against the drums, produce rumbling noises, and, finally, the four shell rattles. "All these were put into the room, for there is no food and property that was obtained as a treasure . . . from the Red Cod. That is the reason why it is said that the red codfish are stingy."

A disconcerting moral, were it not for the fact that, among the Salish, the Swaihwé masks have an opposite nature: they enrich those who own them or who have secured their service. That a mask borrowed by a population from its neighbor should see its attributes inverted in the course of this transfer is a fact rich in lessons to which I will give all my attention later. All the more so since, in a Salish version already mentioned (p. 24), the two sisters and their brother who are self-centered and refuse to get married (that is to say, refuse to open up to the outside world) are said to have a "stomach of stone." Drs. W. G. Jilek and L. N. Jilek-Aall, great experts on Salish culture, have helpfully pointed out to me that this phrase is also present in the songs of the Swaihwé as it is celebrated today, and that it refers to the egotist, he or she who thinks only selfishly, who refuses to act for the good of others and to communicate with them. Thus, the character that the Kwakiutl attribute to their Xwéxwé mask is the same as that which the Salish lend to humans until the mask—which in this case has the opposite virtue—allows them to free themselves from it. It will be remembered that the Kwakiutl Xwéxwé masks have another way of showing their sordid character: they prevent the children from collecting the coins that are randomly flung at them.

On the other hand, the Salish and Kwakiutl masks have a common trait, in that the convulsions gripping the fish (which are linked to underground rumblings and earthquakes) refer directly to those afflicting the Water People of the Salish myths, who have been contaminated by the hero's saliva, and also refer to the masks' acknowledged power to cure convulsions (pp. 22–23). But before looking for an angle from which to approach these problems (since the direct data at my disposal shed no lights), it is advisable that I specify the identity of the fish mentioned in the myth, and try to discover their semantic function.

Commonly called Red Cod or Red Snapper in the myths, these are not really cod, but deep-water rockfish of the species *Sebastes ruberrimus* of the family Scorpaenidae. As the scientific name indicates, they are red, but the same family includes species that are black or otherwise colored. The one I am concerned with comprises very large individual specimens, which may grow to more than one meter in length. It is notable for its spinous fins and scales, which can injure fishermen. It is not surprising, therefore, that the myths of this region frequently refer to villages of red scorpaenids, frightening creatures because of the sharp fin and spines that cover their body. From a more trivial point of view, the meat from these fish is lean and dry, so that, according to the myths, it requires generous dousing with oil, the cause of digestive discomforts which the myths also note and on which I shall not dwell here. This point will be taken up elsewhere (chap. 14). According to the Nootka, Red Cod was a powerful and formidable magician who one day cooked his twelve virgin daughters in an earth oven to feed his guest, Raven, and resuscitated them immediately after. Raven wanted to do the same when he returned the invitation, but his daughters died and Red Cod said he could not bring them back to life.

A myth of the Tsimshian (northern neighbors of the mainland Kwakiutl) links the red scorpaenid to the origin of copper. One night, a prince of celestial origin in "a wonderful garment of shining light," appeared to a jealously guarded chief's daughter who

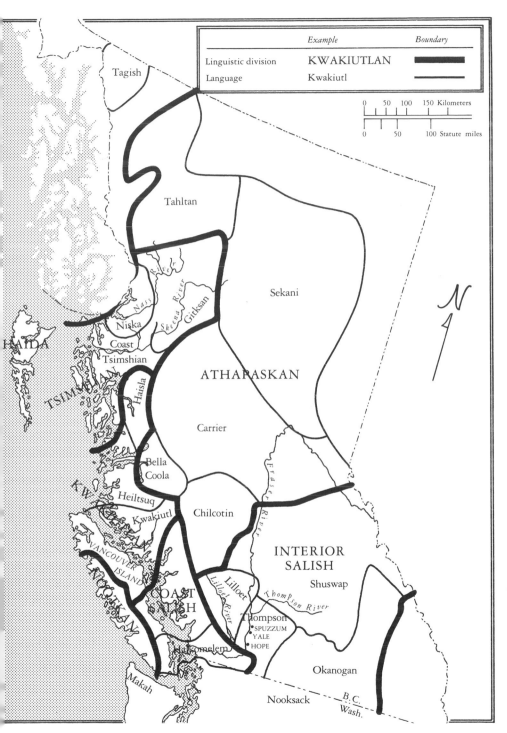

Map 2. Tribal distribution

was languishing for want of a husband. The following night, he sent his slave to fetch her, but she mistook the latter's identity and gave herself to him. The prince then fell back on the younger sister, who was lame and whom he cured of her infirmity. He then took his revenge by succeeding in taking possession of the copper: the precious metal lay on the top of an inaccessible mountain, from which the prince dislodged it with a magic slingshot. The copper came sliding down slowly into the valley where it divided itself to create the deposits we know. The prince and his slave then quarreled during a fishing trip. The prince changed the slave into a red scorpaenid whose stomach pours out of its mouth each time it raises its head. The experts confirm that an internal organ of this fish does come up to its mouth when it is pulled out of the water: "the red snapper," say the Squamish, "turns itself inside out." The prince also changed his sister-in-law into a scorpaenid of the species called Blueside: "the prettiest of all the fish, for it was a princess"; then he went back to the sky with his wife, leaving on earth their two daughters who had since married. One day, the eldest told her husband about the copper deposit created by her father on the upper Skeena. The couple organized an expedition to go and get it, but the project fizzled out: they preferred to stop on the way, to cut down and hew the tree of "sweet smelling scents." The prince's daughter and her husband made a business of it and became rich.

As for the younger daughter, she enlisted her husband in the search for the salmon that transforms itself into copper. He succeeded in finding it, but the fumes exhalating from this "live copper" poisoned him; he died. It was decided to burn the copper, and thus was the discovery made of what is difficult to interpret otherwise than the art of smelting. This episode is all the more mysterious because, generally, knowledge of this art by the Indians of the Pacific Coast is denied: before the introduction of sheet copper by navigators and traders, they had limited themselves to sawing and beating native metal. Anyway, the prince came back down to earth and resuscitated his son-in-law. He taught him that he should be careful of the living copper, and he prohibited its use to all except his daughter's husband and their descendants, who, he said, alone will know how "to kill the live copper" and "to make costly coppers." He showed them, in fact, how one protects oneself against deleterious fumes. Thanks to this knowledge, the couple became fabulously rich.

This myth, founder of privileges claimed by a lineage and concerning the knowledge and working of copper, rests on a series of oppositions and parallelisms. The characters can be sorted into two groups according to their ultimate destination, celestial or aquatic. In this regard, the two sisters who are the protagonists of the second part repeat the two sisters who are the protagonists of the first, because the eldest of the girls discovers an aerial wealth—the tree's perfumes; the youngest discovers aquatic wealth—the copper salmon. From one generation to the other, therefore, the respective affinities of the youngest and the eldest cross each other. Other oppositions are also noted: between the prince and his slave, the beautiful princess and her handicapped sister, the "dead" copper on top of the mountain and the "live" copper in the water, the fragrant odor of the tree and the fatal stench of the copper, both of them sources of wealth, etc.

As the metamorphosis of a perfidious and grasping character—the slave—the red scorpaenid is here again placed on the side of stinginess. This fish is in opposition to the salmon, the live copper which generously enriches its owners, provided they know how to guard against its danger. Although the Tsimshian do not know the Swaihwé or Xwéxwé masks, they do associate, within a pair of opposites, the red scorpaenid, which the Kwakiutl depict as the giver of masks, with the copper that the Salish relate directly to the masks.

Furthermore, the same myth, but told in reverse, exists among the Squamish (of the mainland coast, north of the Fraser), who had the mask under the reported name of Sxaixi. The two daughters of a shaman often went near a lake to find a husband. Black Cod was the first to answer their calls; they refused him because of his big bulging eyes. Next came Rock Cod, a bright and fiery form, but he was too big-mouthed. Then Red Cod showed up, making the waters glow as if a great fire burnt beneath, but he had big eyes and a gaping mouth and they did not want him either. In fact, the young girls were hoping to attract the "luminous son of day," in whom we recognize the alter ego of the prince in the "wonderful garment of shining light" who comes from the sky in the Tsimshian myth, whereas here he emerges from the bottom of the waters. He appeared finally, "a golden form, bright and shining like the sun," and consented to marry the younger sister. But, like the Water People of the Lilloet myth of the Säin-nux masks (see p. 35), the old shaman, father of the two sisters, was using his daughters to lure their suitors in order to destroy them by his magic powers. The hero managed to foil all the traps, and he transformed the house into an enchanted rock within which he imprisoned his father-in-law. This rock exists: if one insults it, a storm breaks out and the culprit sinks with his boat.

Here again, therefore, a hero, who elsewhere is the provider of the copper and who announces himself through his sunlike and metallic dazzle, is put in correlation with and opposition to the scorpaenids. I shall go deeper into the role given to these fish in Part II. The preceding indications are enough to convince me that their intervention in the Kwakiutl myth of the origin of the masks is not fortuitous, and that it is explained by an incompatibility between the Xwéxwé masks and riches, of which the copper is the substance *par excellence* and the symbol. These partial and fragmentary indications, however, are not sufficient to understand that the Swaihwé masks, as I have observed, are brought by the Salish into direct relation with the acquisition of wealth; whereas, among the Kwakiutl directly and among the Tsimshian indirectly, the red scorpaenids—associated with the masks by the Kwakiutl—fill an opposite function. And this, in spite of the fact that, wherever the masks exist, their plastic characteristics remain the same, and the same affinity can be observed between them and earthquakes. In order not to close my brief with this constat of uncertainties, I must stretch my method and discover a novel way out of the impasse where we are provisionally blocked.

4

Meeting the Dzonokwa

Any myth or sequence in a myth would remain incomprehensible if each myth were not opposable to other versions of the same myth or to apparently different myths, each sequence opposable to other sequences in the same or other myths, and especially those whose logical framework and concrete content, down to the smallest details, seem to contradict them. Could we conceivably apply this method to works of art? Yes, if each object, through its contour, decoration, and colors, were the opposite of other objects whose corresponding elements, by their different treatment, contradicted its own, in order to carry a particular message. Should this be true of masks, one would have to grant that, like the words of a language, each one does not contain within itself its entire meaning. The latter is the result of two things: the sense included in the particular term chosen, and the senses (which have been excluded by this very choice) of all the other terms that could be substituted for it.

Let us assume then, as a working hypothesis, that the shape, color, and features that struck me as characteristic of the Swaihwé masks have no intrinsic meaning, or that this meaning is incomplete when considered by itself. All attempts to interpret these elements individually would therefore be wasted. Next, let us as-

sume that this shape, these colors, and these features are insepa-
rable from others to which they are opposed, because they were
chosen to characterize a type of mask, one of whose *raisons d'être*
was to contradict the original. On this assumption, only a comparison of the two types will allow me to define a semantic field
within which the respective functions of each type will be mutually complementary. It is on the level of this total range of
meanings that I must try to place my analysis.

Assuming that there exists a type of mask that stands in opposition and correlation to the Swaihwé, one should, therefore,
knowing this, be able to deduce its distinguishing features from
those I have used when describing the prototype. Let me try this
experiment. Through its accessories and the costume that goes
with it, the Swaihwé mask manifests an affinity for the color white.
The opposite mask will therefore be black, or will manifest an
affinity for dark hues. The Swaihwé and its costume are adorned
with feathers; if the other mask does entail trimmings of animal
origin, these should be in the nature of fur. The Swaihwé mask
has protruding eyes; the other mask's eyes will have the opposite
characteristic. The Swaihwé mask has a wide-open mouth, a sagging lower jaw, and it exhibits an enormous tongue; in the other
type, the shape of the mouth should preclude the display of this
organ. Finally, one would expect that the origin myths, the respective religious, social, and economic connotations of the two
types, will have between them the same dialectical relationships
(of symmetry, of contrast, or of contradiction) as those previously
noted from the plastic point of view alone. If this parallelism can
be proven, it will definitely confirm the initial hypothesis according to which, in a domain such as that of masks (which combines
mythic elements, social and religious functions, and plastic
expressions), these three orders of phenomena, seemingly so het-
erogeneous, are functionally bound together. Hence, they will jus-
tifiably receive the same treatment.

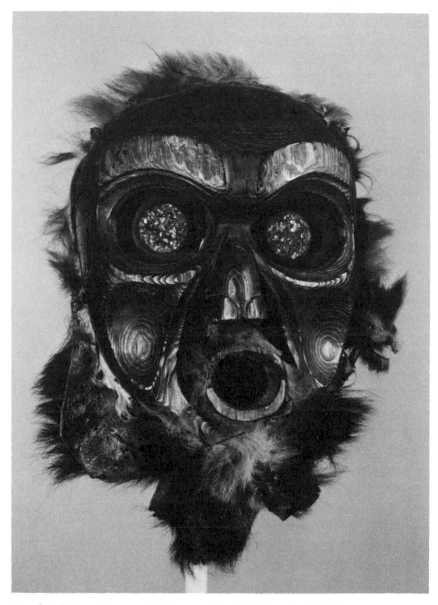

Kwakiutl Dzonokwa mask (Museum für Völkerkunde, Berlin)

Now, no sooner have the conditions this ideal mask should meet been enunciated *a priori* than its existence in reality is recognized. Starting from purely formal requirements, I was in fact describing and reconstructing, with all its plastic characteristics, the mask called Dzonokwa, which the Kwakiutl own among many others, including, let us not forget, the Swaihwé mask (under the name Xwéxwé) borrowed from the Salish. Moreover, Kwakiutl legendary tales establish a connection between the two types: the hero of one of those tales, who will succeed in the peaceful conquest of the Xwéxwé masks, is the son of the supernatural being Dzonokwa; and his magic power derives, above all, from his ability to shout like his parent.

Generally speaking, the term Dzonokwa designates a class of supernatural beings, most often female, but endowed with breasts no matter what their sex. I will, therefore, use the word mainly in the feminine gender. The Dzonokwas dwell far inside the woods; they are savage giantesses, also ogresses, who kidnap the Indians' children to eat them. Yet, the relations they maintain with humans are ambiguous, sometimes hostile, sometimes imbued with a certain complicity. Kwakiutl sculpture favors representations of Dzonokwa; many of its masks are known, being easily recognized by their distinctive traits.

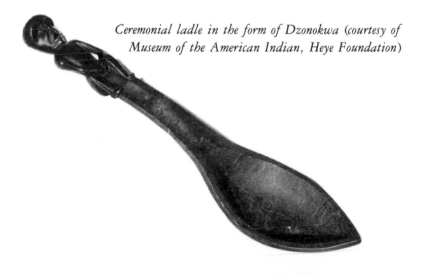

Ceremonial ladle in the form of Dzonokwa (courtesy of Museum of the American Indian, Heye Foundation)

Dzonokwa mask with sunken eyes (British Columbia Provincial Museum, Victoria)

These masks are black, or else the color black predominates in their trimmings. They are, most often, decorated with black tufts representing the hair, beard, and mustache (donned even by the female specimens), and the wearers used to wrap themselves in a black blanket or in a bear skin with dark fur. The eyes, instead of being protuberant and outward-looking like those of the Swaihwé masks, here are pierced through the bottom of hollow sockets, or else they are half-closed. In fact, the concave effect is not limited to the eyes: the cheeks, too, are hollow, as are other parts of the body when Dzonokwa is represented standing. One Kwakiutl myth

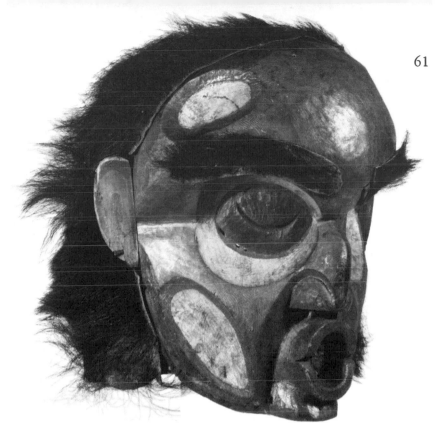

Dzonokwa mask with eyes closed (National Museums of Canada, no. J10153)

has a hero who "saw a hole in the rock on the bank of a river . . . and he saw that the holes were the eyes of a Dzonokwa . . . and he dived into the water in the eyes of the Dzonokwa." According to another myth, the skull of a Dzonokwa served as a washtub. Ceremonial dishes, sometimes enormous, represent the ogress. The main dish is carved out of the belly of the creature who lies on its back with its legs folded. It is accompanied by a veritable table service whose hollow pieces represent the face, the breasts, the navel, and the kneecaps, respectively.

The mouth of the masks and other effigies is not wide open, but, on the contrary, is pushed forward in the pout formed by the monster as it emits its characteristic cry, "uh! uh!" This pursing of the lips precludes any tongue lolling out or even showing at all; but, in the absence of the dangling tongue, all the statues representing Dzonokwa give it decidedly pendulous breasts, hanging down to the ground, it is sometimes said, because they are so heavy.

It will be remembered that, according to the Salish, the prototypes of the Swaihwé masks come from the sky or from the bottom of the water, that is, from up above or down below. The ogres or ogresses, prototypes of the Dzonokwa masks, come, as I have said, from the mountains or the forest, thus from afar. From the functional point of view, the Swaihwé masks represent the ancestors who founded the highest ranking lineages: they incarnate the social order, in contrast with the Dzonokwa who are asocial spirits, and not ancestors (i.e., by definition, the creators of following generations) but kidnappers who put this continuity in jeopardy. In the course of the dances, a masked character tries to blind the Swaihwé by blows with a lance (pp. 17, 26). As I will explain later, Dzonokwa is blind or afflicted with poor sight, and she herself tries to blind (by gluing their eyelids with gum) the children she has stolen and carries in her hod; whereas, the Swaihwé masks are themselves carried in baskets. Finally, while the Swaihwé masks never appear during the sacred winter rites, the Dzonokwa masks participate in them by right.

It should be recalled, at this point, that the Kwakiutl used to divide the year in half. The clan system prevailed during the half named *bakus,* which comprised the spring and summer. Following a four-day carnival, in the course of which the ancestral masks were displayed, the *tsetseka* period opened, which took up the fall and winter. From one period to the other, the proper names, the songs, and even their musical styles changed. The profane clan organization gave way to the religious secret societies. A special social system came into force, defined by the relationships that

Dzonokwa mask with half-closed eyes (British Columbia Provincial Museum, Victoria)

individuals were supposed to have with the supernatural. During this winter period, which was completely devoted to the rites, each secret society proceeded to the initiation of those whose birth and rank qualified them for membership.

The village then split into two groups. The non-initiated formed an audience for whom the initiates appeared in spectacle. One must further distinguish two main categories among the latter. The superior class included the societies of the Seals and the Cannibals: each was subdivided into three grades, which took twelve years to pass through. A little below the two great secret societies was that of the War Spirit. The Sparrows, who constituted the inferior class and may also have included retired old initiates, were themselves subdivided, according to age, into Puffins, Mallards, Killerwhales, and Whales. Parallel societies regrouped the women. At each end of the scale, between the Sparrows and the Seals, a spirit of competition, of hostility even, reigned. The initiation rites offered a theatrical element: the performances were sometimes dramatic, sometimes they verged on a circus, and they required skillful direction involving simulations, acrobatics, and conjuring tricks.

Within this complex system, of which I have drawn merely the general outlines, the Dzonokwa mask, which belonged to the secret society of Seals, played a minor though prescribed role. The dancer who wore it pretended to be asleep, or at least sleepy. A rope was stretched between the dancer's seat and the door to allow him to feel his way around. Also, this personage always arrived a little late to witness the carnage in which the new initiates to the Cannibal secret society pretended to engage. The ritual songs glorify the ogress' power: "Here comes the great Dzonokwa who carries off humans in her arms, who gives us nightmares, who makes us faint. Great bringer of nightmares! Great lady who makes us faint. Terrible Dzonokwa!" And yet, she is too drowsy to dance, loses her way as she circles around the fire and stumbles; she must

Mask of Dzonokwa sleeping (University of British Columbia Museum of Anthropology)

be led back to her seat where she promptly falls asleep. Once awakened, she does not participate actively in the ceremony and when someone points a finger at her she goes back to sleep. One could hardly imagine a more contrasting behavior to that of the Swaihwé (or Xwéxwé) dancers, who, among the Salish, themselves point a finger to the sky to show where they come from (whereas another party points a finger toward the Dzonokwa where she sits, and from where she does not want to budge), and who, among the Kwakiutl, once launched do not want to stop dancing unless they are restrained.

While the Kwakiutl have borrowed the Swaihwé masks from the Salish, the latter share with them the Dzonokwa character or its equivalent. The Fraser groups and the island Comox call her Sasquatch or Tsanaq: a black giantess with bushy eyebrows, eyes deeply sunk in the orbits, long thick hair, a fat-lipped pursed mouth, hollow cadaverous cheeks. The wearer of the mask wraps himself in a black blanket and sways sleepily near the door. Evidently, it is the same character as the Tzualuch of the Lummi, a giant ogress who roams about looking for children to take away in the basket she carries on her back; and the same as the Tal of the island and mainland, an ogress who cooks children in an earth oven and from whose ashes, after she has fallen in and been consumed, mosquitoes (those miniature cannibals) are born. But, though the wearing of the mask created a hereditary privilege, any family could buy the mask provided it had the means to do so. In contrast to the Swaihwé, which was the privilege of a few high-ranking lineages, the purchase of the Tal mask was an expensive, but in every other respect easy, way for upstarts (that is, the "nouveaux riches") to acquire social status. The two types of mask, therefore, are opposed also in this regard.

5

Dzonokwa Myths

Considered purely from the plastic point of view, the Swaihwé mask, which may be described as full of protrusions, is in opposition to the Dzonokwa mask, which is all cavities; but at the same time, the two complement each other almost like a mold and its cast. One foresees that a similar relationship may be observed between their social, economic, and religious functions. Could the same network of oppositions and correspondences extend to the group of myths associated with each type respectively? I have already analyzed and commented upon the mythology of the Swaihwé masks among the Salish. Let me now pursue my investigation among the Kwakiutl, on the subject of the Dzonokwa mask.

A preliminary statement is called for. The tales relating to the Xwéxwé masks (which correspond to the Swaihwé among the Salish) have seemed to belong to two types: one historical, or at least legendary; the other frankly mythic. The first type features the Nimkish and Koeksotenok subgroups, as far as the Kwakiutl are concerned; and the Comox subgroup for the Salish. From the point of view of those who tell them, the setting for these stories, therefore, is a central zone of the island and of the mainland coast, and the part of the island immediately to the south. In the case of the second type of tale, the mythic tales, the opposite is true: they unfold between Nimkish country and Cape Scott, that is to say, between the same central zone of the island and its northernmost part. Putting together these two remarks, it can be said that the origin myths of the Xwéxwé masks evolve entirely on a north–south axis.

By contrast, the myths that feature the Dzonokwa come mainly from Kwakiutl groups, which are scattered along a roughly east–west axis: Nakoatok, Tsawatenok, Tenaktak, Awaitlala, Nimkish, Tlaskenok, to which one might add the northern Nootka. Several of the place names collected by Boas either allude to or refer directly to the Dzonokwa. But, all these individual places—an islet facing the Nimkish River, a site at the bottom of Seymour Inlet, various localities in Knight Inlet, where the myths I will examine unfold—have the same character. In fact, the center of gravity, if it may be so called, of the "myths of Dzonokwa" is situated in Knight Inlet and its surroundings. Knight Inlet is the deepest fjord in Kwakiutl territory. It penetrates far into a mountain mass whose highest peaks reach between 3,000 and 4,000 meters, sometimes higher: Silverthrone Mountain and Mounts Waddington, Tiedeman, Munday, Rodell. Very far to the east lies the most redoubtable and inaccessible region. Thus, the Xwéxwé myths are spread out between two poles: the Comox country, the world of strangers, if not of enemies, on the one hand; and the high seas, the world of the unknown, on the other. The poles of the transverse axis, along which the Dzonokwa myths are distributed, correspond, on the one hand, to the sea, and on the other, to the mainland in its most forbidding and frightening aspects.

Doubtless, these remarks are to be taken with caution. Our data on the Kwakiutl, rich though they may appear when compared with others, are far from exhaustive, and we cannot rule out the possibility that in actual fact the distribution of myths and of geographical names is less clear-cut than I have indicated. But,

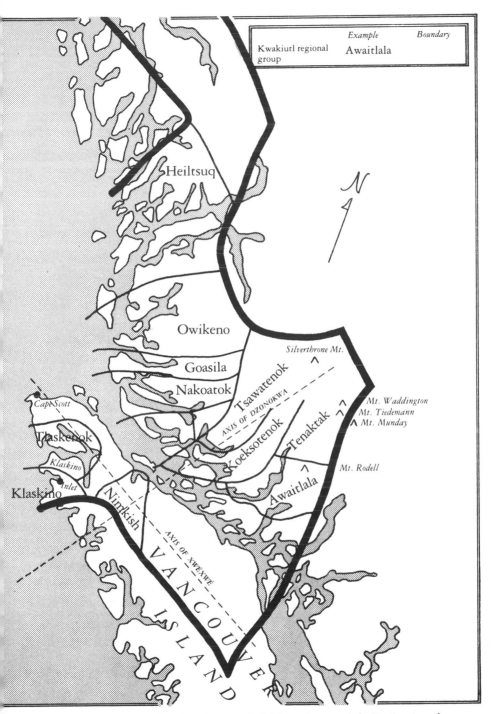

Map 3. Kwakiutl territory showing the axes of the Dzonokwa and the Xwéxwé myths

even if I were to grant a merely exploratory value to the research done by Boas and his followers, the fact that it allows me to allocate the myths concerning the two types of masks along axes going in opposite directions is just as significant.

The Xwéxwé masks' mythology, in itself, has struck me as rather scanty. That of the Dzonokwa is very rich, and to guide me in this labyrinth, a preliminary classification is necessary. The myths that have been collected are distributed along a gamut whose extremities may be qualified, relatively speaking, as weak and strong. Let me begin with an example of the first type.

The Nimkish relate that in order to hush a child who cried constantly, his parents threatened to call the ogress. The child ran away in the middle of the night and Dzonokwa caught him. She dragged him underground; his cries could be heard, but he could not be reached. After vain efforts, the search for him was called off. The ogress took the child far into the interior of the country. But the young captive had cunning: pretending to punch holes in his keeper's ears, from which to hang ornaments, the child pushed her into the fire and burned her. Back at the village, he recounted his adventure. Some of the villagers went to Dzonokwa's place and took possession of all her riches: preserved berries, dried meat, furs, etc. The father of the young hero distributed them in the course of a potlatch.

A myth of the Awaitlala, who lived deep in the interior, on the right bank of Knight Inlet, begins in Hanwati, toward the lower reaches of the fjord. A family there decided to go up the fjord in a boat to fish. But the salmon they put up to dry disappeared one after another. The parents complained bitterly to their young son about his laziness: if only he had set himself the trials prescribed for boys of his age, he might have enjoyed the protection of a spirit which would help his family keep the fruit of their labor.

Stung to the quick, the lad took ritual baths. A spirit came to him and educated him. It also gave him round stones with which the now robust young boy succeeded in killing the fish thieves, who were none other than a band of Dzonokwa. In their lair, the hero and his father found little girl ogresses and accumulated goods: meat, bear and wild goat skins, dried berries, plus all the stolen salmon. They carried this loot, as well as the two little Dzonokwas, to a village apparently belonging to a Kwakiutl group from the east coast of Vancouver Island, beyond the Awaitlala territory. The father took Dzonokwa as his ceremonial name; he invited "all the tribes," offered them a banquet, and, at the peak of the excitement, produced the two Dzonokwas whom he had kept hidden. The entire audience became as though intoxicated by their presence. The young man took advantage of this situation and killed many people. He distributed skins and furs among the few survivors. Back home, he built in front of his house four statues of Dzonokwa to commemorate his exploits.

It is also at Hanwati that a myth of the Tenaktak, neighbors of the Awaitlala, deep inside Knight Inlet, takes place. A hunter and his wife had camped to fish at the entrance of the fjord. At night, they heard and saw a dim shape moving the roof of their shelter to steal fish that had been set to dry underneath. The man took his bow, shot at and hit the creature, who fell in the bushes but managed to escape.

In the morning, the hunter followed its tracks and found the body of a strange creature endowed with great hanging breasts and a round protruding mouth. It was a male Dzonokwa (for this anatomic oddity, see p. 59). The couple paddled upriver to their village. The next day, a party of men going downriver caught sight of a great female Dzonokwa, all in tears on the rocky shore. They went back to the village, reported what they had seen, and the hunter guessed that the creature was mourning her missing congener. The young men, who were very excited, wanted to go look for her immediately, but the eyewitnesses did their best to

Dzonokwa dancer (from Curtis, The North American Indian, *vol. 10, Historical Photography Collection, University of Washington Libraries)*

dissuade them: "Its eyes are enormous," they explained. "There seems to be fire burning inside them. Its head is as big as a storage box." In spite of all this, the young men left, found the Dzonokwa and questioned her; she told them that she had lost her son. Thinking she might kill someone out of sorrow for her son, the youths ran away.

In the village, there lived an ugly young man, a very quiet youth who seldom spoke. He listened to his comrades' story, got up, and, without a word, left in his small canoe. In his turn, he interrogated the Dzonokwa who promised to make him rich if he returned her son to her. He led her to the hunter's shelter and followed the trail to the body, which the Dzonokwa, accompanied by the hero, carried to her place.

The house was very big and filled with goods which the giantess presented to her protégé: dressed skins, dried goat flesh, and a mask that was just like her face. She revived the body of her son with a living water she drew from a basin, and she threw some of it on the homely hero, who became very handsome. But he was sad, he said, because he had lost his parents. She promised that he would know how to bring them back to life. The hero returned to the village with all his riches, celebrated the first winter rite, resuscitated his father and mother with the giantess's magic water. The next day, in front of the whole village, he performed the dance of the Dzonokwa whose riches had allowed him to entertain his guests and shower gifts upon them. At that moment, the huntsman from the beginning of the tale intervened; he laid claim on the dance, which, he maintained, had been conquered through bloodshed. "Oh no," replied the hero, "Dzonokwa gave me this dance. She did not say, 'Take this dance and give it to the one who killed my son.'" And to this day, jealousy and enmity exist between the descendants of these two men.

The Awaitlala and the Tenaktak also recount, and in almost the same terms, that there was once a woman who lived alone with her son. Night after night, their salmon provisions would disappear. The woman made herself a bow and barb-pointed arrows, sat in ambush, saw the Dzonokwa who was lifting up the roofing; she let off a shaft and the giantess was wounded in the breasts. Dzonokwa ran away, pursued by the heroine who found her dead in her house and who cut the head off her remains. The woman saved the skull and bathed her son in it as if in a basin. This treatment lent him unusual vigor. Later, the boy triumphed over various monsters, including a Dzonokwa whom he turned into stone.

Another Kwakiutl group, the Tsawatenok, lived north of Kingcome Inlet. One of their myths features a princess who, soon after puberty, loved to run about the woods at the risk of being carried away by "Dzonokwa of the forest." As a matter of fact, one day she met a big and stout woman who, stammering because she had a speech impediment, invited her to her place. The giantess admired the young girl's plucked eyebrows. The girl promised to make her just as beautiful and received in payment, in anticipation of this service, the ogress' magical garments, which were none other than her puberty clothes. The princess took Dzonokwa to her village where, pretending to put her in the care of the barber, they called a warrior who killed her with a hammer and a stone

Bella Coola Dzonokwa mask (Milwaukee Public Museum of Milwaukee County)

chisel. By order of the princess, the body was decapitated and burnt. The whole village went to the ogress' house, which was filled with such riches as skins, furs, dried meat, and grease. The heroine's father took possession of a mask with a human face surmounted by an eagle in its aerie, called "Nightmare-bringer-nest-mask." These events took place during the profane season. Dzonokwa's provisions were distributed around and the clan responsible for this bounty acquired first rank. It is since that period that at the time of their puberty, young girls wear Dzonokwa's dresses made of goats' hair. I will return to this conclusion.

The Nakoatok of the mainland coast, facing the northern part of the island, tell of twelve children who played on the beach while eating mussels. They harshly drove off a little girl whom they scorned because she was harelipped.* The child saw a Dzonokwa approaching, carrying her basket on her back. Perceiving that she would be the first one taken, she armed herself with a mussel shell; she used it to slit open the bottom of the basket where she lay, and let herself fall to the ground, followed by five other children.

Once she got home, Dzonokwa made preparations to cook the six remaining victims. A very pretty woman, rooted to the floor up to her waist in a corner of the cabin, taught them a magic song to send the ogress to sleep; then there would remain only for the children to push her into the fire. And this is in fact what happened. When Dzonokwa's own children came home, the pretty person told them to sit at the table. The other children, who had been hiding, jeered at them for eating their mother's flesh, and the little ogres ran away. The survivors disinterred their supernatural protectress and took her back to the village.

---

*On the meaning of this infirmity, see my article: "Une préfiguration anatomique de la gémellité," *Systèmes de signes, textes réunis en hommage à Germaine Dieterlen*, Hermann, Paris, 1978, pp. 369–76.

Let me end this survey of the weak forms with the Heiltsuq, or Bella Bella, who are related to the Kwakiutl through language and culture and are settled on the mainland coast between Rivers Inlet and Douglas Channel, facing the southern part of the Queen Charlotte Islands. They say that a little girl who did not stop weeping was entrusted to her grandmother in the hope that the latter would know how to soothe her. A Dzonokwa assumed the appearance of the old woman and stole the child. On the way, the little girl tore off and dropped the fringes of her dress. Her people followed the trail up to the top of a high mountain where the ogress lived. The latter was not there and the little girl was released. Returning home, Dzonokwa noticed that she was gone and set off in pursuit of her. She caught up with the troop of liberators; to neutralize her, they bit their tongues and spat the blood in her direction.

 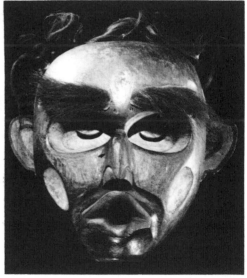

Left: *Heiltsuq Dzonokwa mask with closed eyes (Milwaukee Public Museum of Milwaukee County)*; right: *Dzonokwa mask with half-closed eyes (Milwaukee Public Museum of Milwaukee County)*

She protested that she loved the child and wished to be near her. As a token of her good intentions, she gave her dances to the chief. They succeeded after some effort in chasing her away.

Other Heiltsuq myths give Dzonokwa another name, Kawâka, by which she is occasionally called in this dialect. Taking advantage of a death-dealing epidemic, this ogress stole the cadavers and even able-bodied men, whom she paralyzed by spraying with sparks that she let fly out of her eyes. These were like holes. An Indian wanted to know who the thief was. He let himself be stolen by the ogress and managed to escape. The village went to war against the Kawâka ogresses, all of whom were killed and their bodies burnt, while the hero took possession of all their goods, consisting of copper sheets, furs, and dried meat. Thus enriched, he became a great chief. The Heiltsuq also know versions of myths that vary little from the ones already examined. I have discussed them elsewhere and, in any case, they would not add much to the present brief. Let me therefore move on to the strong versions, which originate mainly from Vancouver Island.

Neighbors of the Nootka, the Tlaskenok, lived in the north of the island, on the western coast. One of their myths relates the visit of a family to a village situated on the shore of Klaskino Inlet, across the water from their own shore. An ogress stole all their children, whom she first blinded by gluing their eyes with gum. The mother of the little ones who had disappeared wept so hard that mucus ran from her nose all the way down to the ground; a child was born out of it. When he grew up, he left in search of his brothers, met a lady rooted to the ground (see p. 75), who told him where the ogress had hidden her heart in order to render herself invulnerable. The hero killed the ogress under the pretext of improving her looks (pp. 74–75), but she came back to life immediately. He killed her for good at last, resurrected his brothers, and rose to heaven.

Still on the island, the Nimkish have a myth relating to the descendants of the first man who lived on earth after the deluge. His son succeeded in marrying the girl he loved by overcoming the reputedly fatal trials set to him by his future father-in-law. They had a son named Giant, master of the Dzonokwa masks, and for a time, the husband of the sun's daughter. Their son presides over the eddies that agitate the ocean.

These myths of the island Kwakiutl have unmistakable affinities with those of their Nootka neighbors, some of whose more coherent versions have been collected. Among these Indians, the ogress is called Malâhas. She stole and killed a woman's children, it is said, by smoking them over the fire; their mother acquired another son, born of her snot, and he set off in search of the ogress. One day, when he had climbed into a tree, the ogress saw his image in the water, fell in love with it, discovered his hiding place, and decided to marry him. More than once, he killed her under the pretext of improving her looks, but she revived each time, as long as he had not found and pierced her heart, which was lodged outside her body. The hero resurrected his brothers by urinating on their dead bodies. Then he rose to heaven to meet his father, he said. Once there, he gave back their sight to two old women in exchange for an itinerary, arrived at his destination, visited his father for a while, and came down again to earth to introduce fish there and put the world in good order. He landed at Dza'wade, "place of the olachen (candlefish)," somewhere near Knight Inlet, freed the imprisoned fish, and married the local chief's daughter, who warned him against her father. The latter did, in fact, seek to kill his son-in-law by submitting him to all sorts of tests. But the young man got the better of him, killed his persecutor, and abandoned his wife to undertake a long peregrination in the course of which he triumphed over adversaries, transforming them into various animals, and gave a normal anatomy to a couple of humans who were incapable of procreating because they had their sexual organs on their foreheads. Finally, he gave the breath of life to some wooden figurines, and this is the origin of present humanity.

For the student of comparative mythology, the interest of these strong versions is all the greater for being found, in barely modified form, in South America. Thus they seem to belong to a very archaic layer of the mythology of the New World. This is not my present concern, it being rather to justify the division of the Dzonokwa myths into two groups. I have qualified as weak those versions that deal exclusively with the squabbles with the ogress, and as strong those that follow this up with a visit of the hero in heaven where, explicitly or implicitly, a conflict sets him against his father-in-law, who is more often than not identified with the sun. Whether the myth states it or implies it, it is, in fact, in order to marry the daughter of the sun that the hero undertakes his ascension. These versions, therefore, involve two female protagonists: first, the ogress, a chthonian creature or one that has an affinity with the subterranean world; then, the sun's daughter, a celestial creature whose home and ancestry all place her on the side of daylight. Granting this, my attention now turns to the already mentioned Tenaktak, who have a myth whose variants achieve a remarkable synthesis of the two aspects.

There was once a young boy who had scabs and sores all over his body. As his sickness was catching, his father, a village chief, decided to abandon him for the good of the other inhabitants. His grandmother took pity on him and left him a small fire and a few provisions. The poor fellow was left alone. Suddenly, a small child came out of his stomach, revealed that he was the cause of his ailment, and asked his "father" to name him Scab. The miraculous child created fish out of hemlock needles gathered from his aunts' graves. But soon all the fish disappeared. Scab sat in ambush, saw the thief, who was none other than Dzonokwa. He shot arrows into her big hanging breasts, gave chase to her, met the ogress' little daughter who led him to her abode. Dzonokwa was there, gravely wounded. Having first tormented her, the hero agreed to care for and cure her, and, in gratitude, he got the little girl as a wife, magic water, and great wealth.

Back at his village after an absence which he thought was short but which had, in fact, lasted four years, he found the bare bones of his father who had since died. His Dzonokwa wife could not see them "because these creatures' eyes are deep set in the orbits," which renders them practically blind.* Thus she had to grope around to find the skeleton, which she resurrected upon touching. Scab soon grew tired of his wife; at his command, Charitonettae (buffle) ducks transported him to heaven. He arrived at the sun and the moon's place and they gave him their daughter in marriage. Later, he came back down to earth with his celestial spouse, rejoined his father and first wife, who, naturally, was jealous of her rival. At first, discord reigned between the two women, then they reconciled. In spite of this, the hero wished to go back to heaven with his second wife, but he fell asleep during the flight and fell to his death. The father and his Dzonokwa daughter-in-law remained alone together on earth.

Two other versions of this myth are known, also collected by Boas, from the same informant, but with an interval of thirty-two years. According to the older version, after the hero had fallen from the sky and died, his Dzonokwa wife resuscitated him; they lived on earth as a good couple. In the other version, where the sick child abandoned by its family is a girl (which makes it more plausible that an offspring should come out of her entrails), Scab's two wives, who hated each other, leave him. He killed himself while attempting to rejoin his favorite in the sky. His father-in-

---

*That is the reason why the traditional Dzonokwa statues have hollow sockets or half-closed eyes. Present-day sculptors seem to have lost interest in this essential characteristic of the ogress. They represent her with wide-open eyes, doubtless to accentuate her ferocious aspect.

law, the sun, resurrected him and he resumed his conjugal life with his celestial spouse.

Thus, the problem of the impossible reconciliation of poles that are too far apart (represented, respectively, by the terrestrial and nocturnal spouse, and the celestial and luminous spouse) is resolved differently in each version. Ineffectual mediator, the hero finds himself ultimately separated from the two poles he had thought he could unite and he dies (version 1); or else, he separates himself definitely from one of the poles and remains joined to the other, which is, according to the case, either the terrestrial pole (version 2) or the celestial pole (version 3). The unrealizable simultaneous union with wives who are too distant from one another is in sharp contrast with the marriage to a reasonably distant woman, which is made possible, in the Salish myths of the Fraser, by the Swaihwé masks that are given in dowry by her brother. This successful marriage ends an almost incestuous intimacy between siblings, just as, in one version here, the broken marriage entails an almost incestuous intimacy between the father-in-law and the daughter-in-law. I have emphasized elsewhere the analogy between the story of Scab and the Greek myth of Adonis, as reinterpreted by Marcel Detienne. But it is on another analogy, this one internal to the American myths, that it is fitting to dwell here. For in all those analyzed since the beginning of this book, the stinking hero (characterized as covered with sores in the Fraser valley, as well as north of Knight Inlet), the crying child, the ugly or lazy—even slothful—adolescent, or else the lively but disobedient youth, who therefore—for reasons that vary from place to place—proves insupportable to his family, are all one and the same person. His appearance alone changes, since the myths content themselves with shifting his blemish (the inverted sign of his election) from the physical to the moral plane.

6

The Clue to the Mystery

Among the Southern Kwakiutl, Dzonokwa also appears in pot-latches. The individual representing her carries a basket on his back in which are stuffed decorated copper objects of a kind I will describe later (chap. 11), and to which I shall refer from now on as "coppers." He hands them over to the chief whenever the latter needs them. At the most solemn moment, the chief himself wears a Dzonokwa mask called Geekumhl. Its carving is more carefully done. Instead of her usual stupid face, the giantess is given a very firm and authoritative expression. The chief who wears the mask incarnates Dzonokwa; and thus it is she who sells or gives away complete coppers, or who first cuts them into pieces with a hard-wood chisel whose handle also represents her.

As a matter of fact, all the myths relating to Dzonokwa make her the owner of fabulous riches, which she spontaneously offers to her protégés, or which humans seize after killing her or chasing her away. There is yet another way of obtaining them: Dzonokwa has a baby who, she says, never cries (in contrast with the children she steals). Anyone who succeeds in surprising her and her off-spring, and who, by pinching the latter, causes it to cry, may receive marvelous presents from the ogress: magic canoe, water of life, and death bringer. When one calls on Dzonokwa unexpect-

Above: *Kwakiutl Dzonokwa mask, Geekumhl type (University of British Columbia Museum of Anthropology)*; right: *modern totem pole of Dzonokwa with wide-open eyes, holding infant (B. C. Provincial Museum, Victoria)*

edly, one often finds her busy carving a canoe out of a tree trunk; but, because of her blindness or bad sight, she invariably makes a hole in her unfinished piece. This clumsiness is not very surprising given that this personage seems earthbound: if Dzonokwa takes every opportunity to steal fish from the Indians, it is because she herself is deprived of water produce. As described in the myths, her riches seem to have a terrestrial origin exclusively—coppers, furs, dressed skins, the grease and meat of quadrupeds, dried berries: "Oh, how much property one saw there! But there was no food from the rivers and streams . . . as all she had to offer her guests was dried meat." Yet, there is sometimes a mention of a "Dzonokwa of the sea"; a ceremonial dish shows her next to three other figures representing fish, in a house whose ancestral spirit, which is painted on its facade, is a whale. But the records also mention a "forest whale." In both cases, the paradoxical assigning of a territorial or marine being to its opposed habitat seems to refer less to the earth or the sea in the strict sense than to a subterranean world whose entrance, as we shall see, opens in the uttermost depths of the ocean.

There exist monumental sculptures in the likeness of Dzonokwa. A statue more than seven meters high shows her with hands outstretched, ready to receive the property when the wife's family arrives to pay the marriage debt. I have already mentioned the gigantic dishes, carved out of the abdomen of an ogress, two or more meters tall, who is represented lying on her back with folded knees. Smaller dishes occupy the sites of the face, the breasts, and the kneecaps. Thus, all these parts of the body, which are normally convex, are turned into so many cavities (see p. 61).

An admirable but seldom quoted text of Barrett's specifies that guests were afraid to be served in such dishes. When they learned of their host's intention to use them, they prepared themselves for any eventuality. They all bedecked themselves with ornaments and body paintings that gave them a ferocious appearance, then they sat according to their individual ranks, and, with mixed feelings of apprehension and some belligerency, watched out for the arrival of the dish. Came the moment when the young men belonging to

Dzonokwa with outstretched arms (from Curtis, The North American Indian, *vol. 10, Historical Photography Collection, University of Washington Libraries)*

the host's clan let out ritual shouts and lifted the dish, which was hidden outside, and introduced it into the house; the head, with the chief's son riding on its neck, appeared in the door. Immediately, the speaker for the ranking visiting tribe ordered the bearers to stop. Singing, he promised a feast: "This we do to keep the head of the Tsonokwa facing towards us because we are the head tribe." Again the young men lifted the dish, they advanced a short distance, and the speaker of the number two tribe stopped them in his turn, he, too, promising a feast. The same incident was repeated until all the invited tribes had spoken. The dish was then put down with its stern toward the door, unless one of the tribes was too poor to promise a feast. In that case, the stern was turned to point in its direction. This precipitated a fight between the host tribe and the one they had thus disgraced. The silent ones tried to throw some part of the dish into the fire, or else the adversaries tried to jostle each other into the main dish: the supreme insult, since it imposed eternal indignity on the one or several who were "washed in my feasting dish." So, the movements of this utensil were anxiously watched. Should the young men be a bit careless in carrying the dish and have the stern pointing, even slightly, toward one of the tribes, a warning was sounded. If the error was not corrected immediately, the young men were roughly handled. Finally, the big dish was set to rest in the right position, that is to say, behind the fire, with its head pointing toward the center post of the back of the house. The chief successively struck the pieces of the service corresponding to the head, the right breast, the left breast, the navel, the right knee, and the left knee. The plates were divided among the tribes according to the order of precedence, and then ordinary dishes and ladles were brought out

Group of ceremonial dishes representing Dzonokwa's body parts (Milwaukee Public Museum of Milwaukee County)

to distribute the food served from the abdominal cavity. An official "counter" took charge of the operations, deciding and announcing the number of dishes assigned to each group of guests. The guests ate very little on the spot, most of the food being meant to be taken home. Only seal, whale, grease, berries, and other vegetable products could be served in the ceremonial plates. Land animals, fish, and clams or other shellfish were not allowed because they were common foods, acceptable at small feasts and served in common dishes only.

All these facts show the link between the character of Dzonokwa and accumulated or distributed wealth. There are other links to which attention should also be drawn: thus, the connection established in one myth between Dzonokwa and pubescent girls, to explain the fact that their ritual clothes imitate hers. These clothes consist of a piece of bark and narrow straps of woven goat's hair, which hug the young person's body tightly, precluding practically all movement. A text describes a princess in this condition; at this time, she is given a provisional name meaning "Sitting-still-in-the-house." Indeed, she crouches, immobile, with her knees pressed against her chest. Her daily meal is limited to four small pieces of dried salmon, dipped in a little oil, which the shaman woman who looks after her slips between her lips; her drink consists of a little water, which she sucks up through a tube of bone. To keep her mouth small, she must open it as little as possible, and when she drinks, she may swallow four times only so as not to put on weight; only then is she allowed to eat, chewing slowly. As long as her seclusion lasts, she can wash only one day in four. After one month, she is released from her straps, her eyebrows are pulled out (p. 74), and her hair is cut. The shaman woman places the wool straps on the branches of a yew tree.

If the princess' father owns a copper, he places this precious object on the right of his daughter so that she may, subsequently, easily obtain the ones she will carry on her back to her future husband. The ritual song of the pubescent girl is addressed to her future suitors: "Be ready, O chiefs' sons of the tribes! to be my husbands; for I am mistress . . . I, mistress, come to be your wife, O princes of the chiefs of the tribes! I am seated on coppers, and have many names and privileges that will be given by my father to my future husband. . . ."

As a matter of fact, as Boas has shown, marriage among the Kwakiutl was a kind of purchase conducted on the same principles and by the same rules as those for a copper. However, Boas adds, it should not be concluded that the husband buys only his wife. The latter's clan also buys out his right to the future children of the couple, and whatever the son-in-law acquires is not for his own use, but for that of his successors. When they are born, the wife's family offers the husband payments even more considerable than those it received at the time the bride was given away. These counterdues are meant to "repurchase" the wife, so that if she decides to remain with her husband, this will be of her own free will and, so to speak, for nothing. The son-in-law, therefore, often responds with a new payment, to secure for himself a right to his wife. The link between marriage transactions and copper transactions also flows from the fact that before and after her wedding, the woman strives to amass coppers; she will tie four of them on a stick, which she offers to her husband.

These practices shed light on the reason why Dzonokwa gives pubescent girls the ritual costume that had first belonged to her. The myths and rites have shown us two aspects of the personality of the ogress. First of all, she is a kidnapper, but she is also the holder and dispenser of the means for giving the potlatch, among the most prized items of which are the coppers. An articulated mask in three parts, when pulled apart through manipulation of the strings, reveals a copper background, which thus seems to stand for the ogress' very essence.

But, upon reaching nubility (that is, marriageable age), the

Kwakiutl Dzonokwa mask with copper base and hinged eyes and jaw, shown closed and open (facing page) *to reveal copper background* (*University of British Columbia Museum of Anthropology*)

young girl becomes comparable to Dzonokwa, and this on two counts. She offers the coppers to her future husband, and she steals from him, in advance, the children to be born from their union. From the point of view of the bride's family, everything happens as if, indeed, the children should belong to the wife's group rather than the husband's. Looked upon from a certain perspective, the

opposition between the two roles filled by the ogress underlies her
unsociable character; but, from a different perspective, the young
girl would seem to fill a social role and an economic function that
give her the appearance of a *tamed* Dzonokwa: upon entering the
conjugal state, she behaves toward her own kin in the same fashion
as Dzonokwa, but reverses the direction of the exchanges in their
favor. The ogress steals children from humans and, willy nilly,
cedes the coppers to them; by contrast, the young bride takes her
family's coppers away from them, and brings the children to them.

This presentation of the facts explains the affinity, required by the myths, between Dzonokwa and the young girl of marriageable age, but, by stressing the maternal right, it seems to contradict today's prevalent views on the social organization of the Kwakiutl. Indeed, most writers estimate that these Indians had bilateral descent, inflected by a quite pronounced patrilineal bias. I believe, however, that the true nature of Kwakiutl institutions has not been understood by observers and analysts, and that, within them, the matrilineal and patrilineal principles are in active competition at all levels. The problem is too vast to be dealt with here, and I prefer to postpone its full discussion, which is the object of chapter 13 in Part II. If my interpretation is correct, it is rather toward her in-laws that the wife behaves like a true Dzonokwa: stealing the future children from her husband, and giving him in return material and immaterial wealth, of which the coppers are at once the substance and the symbol.

Similarly, among the Salish, the Swaihwé masks, which are the source and symbol of wealth, were transmitted by the woman to her husband. We have seen (pp. 19–20; also cf. pp. 160–61) that the mask has spread in this way from the groups of the Fraser Valley all the way down to Musqueam in the estuary, then north and south along the coast, and across the water to Vancouver Island. By the same device, the island people transmitted it to the Southern Kwakiutl.

On the other hand, the link between Swaihwé and riches, which is so obvious among the Salish, is inverted by the Kwakiutl, who lend their Xwéxwé masks a diametrically opposed function. Indeed, the Kwakiutl masks are avaricious, and they prevent the spectators from enriching themselves instead of helping them to do so (pp. 43, 49). As a consequence of the preceding considerations, which have allowed us to see in Dzonokwa the source of all wealth, a correlational and oppositional relationship thus seems to exist between the two types of masks and the functions respec-

Right: *Cowichan Swaihwé mask* (courtesy of Museum of the American Indian, Heye Foundation); overleaf: *Kwakiutl Dzonokwa mask* (University of British Columbia Museum of Anthropology, photograph by Johsel Namkung)

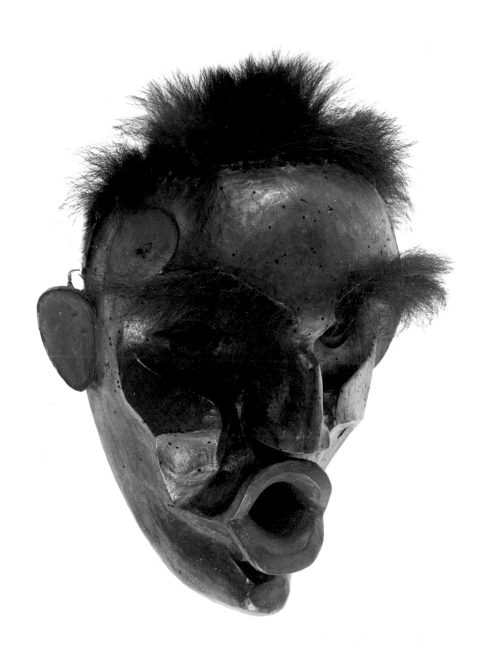

tively assigned to them. The canonical formula for this relationship may be stated as follows:

When, from one group to another, the plastic form is preserved, the semantic function is inverted. On the other hand, when the semantic function is retained, it is the plastic form that is inverted.

Let me recapitulate. Except for stylistic differences, all the plastic characteristics of the Swaihwé masks are found in the Xwéxwé masks of the Kwakiutl, but the latter, being avaricious instead of generous, fill a function opposite to that of the former. By contrast, the Dzonokwa mask (which dispenses riches like the Swaihwé and, like it, transfers its wealth from the wife's family to the husband's) has plastic characteristics, which, down to the smallest details, constitute a systematic inversion of the Swaihwé mask's characteristics.

I have thus demonstrated that beings as different in appearance as the Salish Swaihwé and the Kwakiutl Dzonokwa, which no one would have dreamed of comparing, cannot be interpreted each for itself and considered in isolation. They are parts of a system within which they transform each other. As is the case with myths, the masks (with their origin myths and the rites in which they appear) become intelligible only through the relationships that unite them. The white color of the Swaihwé trimmings, the black color of the Dzonokwa mask, the protruding eyes of the one versus the concave eyes of the other, the lolling tongue and the pursed mouth, all these traits mean less in and of themselves than they do as, one might say, diacritical signs. The attribution of each feature to this or that supernatural being is a function of the way in which, within a pantheon, these beings are opposed to each other in order to assume complementary roles.

This analysis could end here, since it had as its sole object this demonstration. It is, however, possible to extend the paradigm and, by lengthening the search, attain an even wider system, within which the one I have just outlined assumes its place.

Overleaf: *Kwakiutl Xwéxwé mask (University of British Columbia Museum of Anthropology, photograph by Bill Holm)*; left: *Dzonokwa mask, Geekumhl type (Milwaukee Public Museum of Milwaukee County)*

7

In Search of Wealth

Dzonokwa owns the copper, and the myths tell how humans obtained it from her and were thus able to give the first potlatches. But where does the precious metal come from? The question is answered in other myths that reveal the place that certain lucky people were able to reach, where they received the copper, bringing it back to their fellow citizens without passing through the intermediary of the ogress.

The Kwakiutl thought of the ocean as an immense stream running northward. Also in the North (other texts say in the West; in any case, in the high seas), is the mouth of the earth through which the dead descend to the country of the ghosts. When the tide ebbs, the sea fills the underworld; when it rises, it empties it. Over this at once aquatic and chthonian world, peopled with monsters and marine animals, reigns a powerful divinity: Komogwa, master of all riches. His palace is made entirely of copper, as is the furniture, including a sofa on which he stretches his corpulent body (most myths describe him as a fat invalid), and his boat. He keeps loons as guards and seals as servants, and he has inexhaustible supplies of goods.

A blind princess, lost at sea by her slaves, one day berthed alongside his palace after a perilous journey afloat at the mercy of

94

the currents. The god's son married her and gave her back her sight with a miracle water. Four sons were born to them. After they grew up, they returned to their maternal family, traveling on a self-paddling copper canoe, laden with coppers and other gifts.

According to another myth, a princess was given in marriage by her parents to a stranger with a dignified air who turned out to be a bear. A woman prisoner of this Blue Beard warned the princess: she must abstain from eating her husband's food, and, above all, from giving herself to him. But one day sleepiness overtook her, and she allowed a kiss; at once she grew a beard that reached down to her chest. The unfortunate girl managed to escape in the ogre's only boat. The current carried her to the shore opposite where her abductor lived. There was a house there; she entered it. A personage who was lying on his back welcomed her, married her, and rid her of her superfluous hair. It was Komogwa, whose dwelling is called House-of-Happiness. Indeed, at first the young woman was happy there and she gave her husband four children, alternately boys and girls. But in the end she grew homesick; feeling sorry for her, Komogwa sent her back to her village with costly coppers, all kinds of provisions, ceremonial dishes, and various presents. The Kwakiutl myths tell of other visits to Komogwa by a hero who is a shaman in search of supernatural powers, or else by a young man seeking death because he had been humiliated. In both cases, the hero lets himself slide or be carried away to the bottom of the waters, and he arrives at the house of Komogwa, who has been made infirm by a wound that the visitor alone manages to heal. He is rewarded with riches and magic gifts and returns home.

Let me return for a moment to the bearded princess of the second myth. The adventure unfolds along a horizontal axis with, on one side, the land of her bear husband, and on the other, the high seas where she is welcomed by the marine god. This story of a woman between two men is counterbalanced by another about a

Above: *Mask of Komogwa's wife* (*University of British Columbia Museum of Anthropology*); right: *Kwakiutl mask of Komogwa, master of wealth, with aquatic bird on his head* (*University of British Columbia Museum of Anthropology*)

man between two women: this tale develops along a vertical axis, between the earth (and even the sky since it features a bird) and the chthonian world. The chief of a coastal village one day caught a mysterious white swan, which gave out a strong smell of copper. When the bird changed itself into a woman, he married her though she refused to say who she was and where she came from. One day, she lured her husband far inland, under the pretext that she wanted to have him marry a second wife, daughter of a chthonian personage. Through the hole that he used to communicate with the outside world, the latter handed over to his visitor a baby and a chamber pot filled with urine. The hero, taken aback by the prospect of having to carry this infantile fiancée for months on his back, politely declined the offer. That was too bad, because if only he had sprinkled the baby with the pot's contents, the infant would have grown quickly into a pretty young woman. The first wife rebuked her husband, but in fact she was less concerned with acquiring a co-wife than she was with securing possession of the dressed caribou skins making up the dowry, which were quickly put in a safe place. She used them to transform her husband's boat into a submarine; this allowed her to escort her husband to Komogwa, who, it is then revealed, is her father. She brought him the terrestrial goods of which he is deprived: hemlock poles, roots, twigs of the cedar tree, and so on. For though Komogwa owns the salmon, he does not have the ligneous materials needed to build fishing weirs. The hero stayed with his father-in-law for a while, then went back to his people with his wife and son, laden with sumptuous presents.

Three aspects of these myths are of special interest. One of the princesses made welcome by Komogwa was blind; and it is also said that Komogwa ate human eyes, whose original owners, it can be assumed, were consequently deprived of sight. Pacific Coast myths often speak of a supernatural child who, every night, tears out and eats the eyes of the inhabitants of the village where he finds himself. According to the Tsimshian, neighbors of the Kwakiutl, this child was the son of a prince and of a lake-dwelling divinity. The whole population, save his father and his father's sister, perished as the result of his criminal operations. Crushed by the reproaches of the prince, her husband, the woman of the lake promised to make him very rich, and she transformed her sister-in-law into Lady Wealth, a character I shall consider again soon; all those, she said, who hear her child cry will become rich. The brother and sister went their separate ways, he to the north, she to the south. As for the woman of the lake, changed into a siren, she took up residence at the bottom of the seas.

It is known that there was a Haida totem pole that stood at Tanu, a copy of which (of native manufacture) adorns the entrance to the British Columbia Provincial Museum in Victoria. Among other mythical figures, it represents a "sea chief" with dangling eyes: every night, his eyes would drop out of their sockets; his friends would put them back in place at meal times so that he could see what he was eating. As conceived by the sculptor, the useless eyes are decorated with little faces, and, hanging at the ends of long stems, they drop down to the feet of the figure. Nothing could contrast better with the blazing eyes of the Swaihwé masks, which are solidly fixed on their cylindrical base as if to underline the fact that, unlike human eyes which can be torn out, or the "sea chief's" eyes which are loose, theirs are immovable. Furthermore, the Swaihwé masks constitute a means for a brother to arrange a good match for his sister, that is, to marry her off suitably, into a group that is foreign, but close.

By contrast, all the myths directly or indirectly built around the theme of the villagers with the plucked-out eyes seem to refer to a marriage to someone too far away, be it the Komogwa who lives at the end of the world, or the woman of the lake who dwells at the bottom of the waters. These risky marriages may turn out to the advantage or the detriment of those who contract them—doubtless, we are not the only ones who conceive of Fortune as a blind or blinding goddess. Even though this analogy may seem hazardous, it nonetheless remains that the inversion already noted when one goes from the Salish to the Kwakiutl, is maintained between these two peoples when we view it from a different angle: the Salish associate measured exogamy and reasonable enrichment with good sight, the Kwakiutl associate immoderate exogamy and extravagant accumulation of wealth with bad sight.

The other princess is not blind; but, from her marriage to a bear (which is another form of extreme exogamy), she earns a beard, a premonitory sign of her eventual transformation into a Dzonokwa, a character noted for its hairiness. When her husband's boat moors, she cannot climb the bank because it is too steep. He then takes her on his back; this is what Dzonokwa does with the children she steals, but it is what the hero of the subsequent myth refuses to do for his infantile spouse. Then the bear husband, carrying his wife, pulls himself up along the strong root of a conifer, which, uncovered by the gullying, reached all the way down to the sea (whereas, in the other myth, roots are precisely what is lacking in Komogwa's riches). All these facts suggest that Komogwa, Dzonokwa, and humans form a system. Each term is defined by ownership of two types of wealth and the absence of a

"Dzonokwa of the Sea," painting by Mungo Martin (British Columbia Provincial Museum, Victoria)

third one. Komogwa has copper and fish but not forest products. Dzonokwa has the last and copper, but is deprived of fish, which she must steal from humans. Finally, humans have fish and forest products, but until they get it from Dzonokwa, they do not have copper.

	Copper	Forest products	Fish
Komogwa	+	−	+
Dzonokwa	+	+	−
Humans	−	+	+

This triangular system, which connects and opposes humanity to two types of supernatural beings, probably explains the affinities one observes between Komogwa and Dzonokwa. Both are cannibals. There is a Dzonokwa of the sea, although this character is essentially terrestrial; but, even when she dwells at the top of a mountain, she lives in a very deep lake there in the company of sea lions and otters. In truth, Dzonokwa represents mainly a chthonian personage, and the same may be said of Komogwa, who is described as a spirit residing at the bottom of the sea but who sometimes, like Dzonokwa, lives deep in the mountains. In fact, a great statue of Dzonokwa stands in front of his house, where posts support carved beams representing sea lions. To an Indian whom he has received, Komogwa gives, before sending him away, coppers, plus a mask and receptacle, both of which are made in the likeness of Dzonokwa; or, according to another version, a totem pole with a representation of Dzonokwa in its lower portion.

Let me go further into the last of the three aspects mentioned above. A myth that I have already summarized attributes a daughter to Komogwa (p. 97): a princess who appears first in the shape of a copper-smelling swan, and who, later, having reassumed her human form, gives birth to twins of opposite sex.

The little girl dies in infancy, and the boy exudes the same odor as his mother. It is difficult to ascertain if this princess is the same one as the daughter given to Komogwa by other traditions. But whether she is the same or not, her name is Kominaga, wife and accomplice of Baxbakwalanuxsiwaé, "Cannibal-who-lives-at-the-north-end-of-the-world." By the virtue of this, she plays an important role during initiation into the Cannibal secret society, which is, it will be remembered, the highest ranking secret society of the Kwakiutl.

The smell of copper, distinguishing characteristic of the daughter and grandson of Komogwa, is called *kîlpala* in Kwakiutl, a term which is also applied to the smell of salmon. This sidelight reminds me of the relationship of equivalence between copper and salmon already in evidence in the Salish myths (pp. 35–38), but there is more to this connection. The Swaihwé masks' origin myths of the island Salish compare the characteristic smell of one of the protagonists to the noise of the rattle he carries: indeed, according to the different versions, the smell or the noise might scare away the salmon (p. 20). As for the myths of the mainland Salish of the Fraser and the coast, they have as hero a boy afflicted with a malodorous leprosy. He catches a salmon that turns into a frog; in his predicament, this proves to be the last straw. Or else, it is the disease itself that escapes from his body in the shape of frogs; whereas the Kwakiutl, in a very similar tale, introduce a she-toad who is both healer and dispenser of copper (p. 37).¹ Here, then, we have a quadripartite system that brings into close relationship a smell (described everywhere as hard to bear, even when it emanates from such a sought-after material as copper: it is said of Komogwa's son-in-law that "he could not endure the strong smell of the boy, for he smelled very strong of copper"), the copper itself, frogs, and salmon. I will return to this connection.

Whether Kominâga is the same daughter of Komogwa who figures elsewhere, or whether she is another one, it must be admitted that little is known about this Rich Lady. The Heiltsuq, or Bella Bella, who are close kin of the Kwakiutl, called her by the same name and are a little more explicit. They recount that a young woman one day stepped on the dung of a bear. Disgusted, she hurled insults at the animal. The latter immediately appeared, and asked her what kind of excrement she herself produced to dare criticize his. She coolly replied that hers were mother-of-pearl and copper. Challenged to prove it, she crouched down, pretended to defecate, and slipped one of her bracelets underneath her. The enraptured bear married her, and took her to his residence where the carved posts represented Thunderbird perched on the head of a Kawâka (the Bella Bella equivalent of Dzonokwa, see p. 77). Soon, the woman gave birth to a bear cub. Later, her brothers succeeded in releasing her and in taking possession of the accessories pertaining to the "dance of the cannibal bear." Back at the village, the eldest brother and the sister disappeared soon after; then they came back, he as the cannibal dancer, she as Kominâga.

The marriage of a supernatural woman and Cannibal-who-lives-at-the-north-end-of-the-world, or of a human and a bear, are examples of different degrees of immoderate exogamy. The Tlingit, who have the same myth as the Bella Bella (in fact, the tale is known to all the coastal peoples), add, in the way of commentary, that ever since then, when women see the bear's spoor, they shower praise upon it and beg the bear not to ravish them. To this example of extreme exogamy is opposed what one may consider as its lowest limit: the too-close association between a brother and a sister, which the Bella Bella illustrate in the concluding episode of their myth. The Bella Coola, who are a Salish people isolated between the Kwakiutl and the Bella Bella, have a variant that confirms this interpretation. According to them, the bear's wife changed herself into a she-bear who murdered her whole family except her brother and sister, who, in turn, managed to kill her and became an incestuous couple. In pursuit of my investigation,

Left: *Kwakiutl copper-cutting stand in the form of a bear (University of British Columbia Museum of Anthropology)*; above: *Haida ceremonial hat showing the children of Property Woman as frogs abandoning the Queen Charlotte Islands (Museum für Völkerkunde, Berlin)*

I thus always fall back on the same theme: that of arbitrating between marriage that is too near and marriage that is too distant.

While a certain mist envelops Komogwa's daughter or the "Rich Lady" of the Kwakiutl, information is more forthcoming on Lady Wealth, her equivalent among their Haida and Tlingit neighbors. The former call her Djilaqons, the leading supernatural creature among those that haunt the headsprings of coastal rivers and are mistresses of the fish. The Eagle clan of the Haida trace their origin to an ancestor who captured Djilaqons and married her (see p. 96). A good time later, fishermen one day found a copper-skinned frog in the river; they tortured it, tried in vain to burn it, but it was they who perished. Djilaqons then appeared, carrying a cane. As the Kwakuitl say of Dzonokwa, she stammered: thus she was afflicted with a problem of acoustical communication, parallel to the problem of visual communication (or redoubling it in the case of Dzonokwa) implied by defective vision (see pp. 62, 80). Djilaqons caused a fiery rain to fall, which destroyed the culprits' village and all its inhabitants. Her daughter, the only one spared, gathered quantities of coppers in the ashes*; this rich dowry allowed her to marry a prince, with whom she went to settle in Tsimshian country (on the mainland, facing the Queen Charlotte Islands where the Haida live). Thus, while it is true that she married in a foreign country, it was at a reasonable distance, which is the kind of marriage noble families sought in real life.

Djilaqons also bears the name Skîl-dja'a-dai, "Lady of Properties," and, in addition, the word *skîl* designates a supernatural bird. No one has ever seen her, but whoever hears her sound, like the sound of bells or of metal sheets being slapped against each other, becomes rich. Wealth is also promised to those who see Djilaqons, especially if one succeeds in seizing a flap from her mantle, or if one hears her child crying. The Kwakiutl say the same thing about Dzonokwa, when her child is made to weep by being pinched, though its mother claims that it never weeps. It seems, therefore, that among these Indians, several of the traditional attributes of Lady Wealth are taken over by Dzonokwa—one could easily dub her a Lady Wealth on a smaller scale were she not a giantess—and that the lesser importance they give to Rich Lady is explained by this fact.

---

*It is notable that, in the Salish (Halkomelem) dialects of the lower Fraser, the word for copper is *squal,* whose root means "cooked" or "burnt."

Painted panel in a Haida house, representing Qonoqada (from Swanton, Contributions to the Ethnology of the Haida)

The Haida and the Tlingit have an equivalent of Komogwa (Qonoqada or Gonaqadet). The status of the marine monster called Wasgo by the Haida is less clear, although, like Gonaqadet, he dies trapped in a split tree. The word Gonaqadet has two meanings: it designates first a marine monster who procures immense riches for those who catch sight of it, and whose daughters (the equivalents of the Haida Djilaqons) are, according to the Tlingit, mistresses of coastal rivers. It will be recalled that, among the Kwakiutl, Kominâga (Rich Lady) may also be Komogwa's daughter. On the other hand, the Tlingit call outsiders whom they have invited to a feast, Gonaqadet. For they will soon have to return the invitation in an even more lavish way, and their visit, like that of Gonaqadet, announces all sorts of bounties. This correlation reminds me of the great statue of Dzonokwa photographed by Curtis in Kwakiutl country, whose outstretched arms greet the anticipated gifts due from the wife's family in return for those already given by the husband's family (see p. 85).

The Lady Wealth of the Tlingit, Lenaxxidek, is featured in a plot which is very similar to that of a Tsimshian myth already cited (p. 97). One day, an Indian stole a baby girl from her mother, who was an aquatic divinity. But, every night, the baby dug out and ate the eyes of everybody in the village. Only a sick and isolated woman, with her child, escaped from the little ogre whom she killed with her walking stick (an attribute of the Haida Lady Wealth, see p. 104). She became Lenaxxidek. Whoever hears her child cry and carries it away should consent to return it only in exchange for the coppers she owns. She will scratch the kidnapper with her copper fingernails and alert him to the fact that if he gives anyone a scab from his wounds, which will be slow to heal, that person will become rich, which is in fact what did happen.

Moreover, Lady Wealth leaves a trace of her passage: she has the curious habit of arranging shells, from the mussels she eats, in regular order inside one another. A Kwakiutl ceremonial cane, trimmed with small superimposed coppers, illustrates a legend about shells that have been gathered on a beach and changed into coppers. In other myths of the region, scabs from sores, or snot, placed in shells of gradually increasing size, grew and became a child destined to great things. As for the Tlingit, they prohibited the gathering of shells abandoned on beaches. To contravene this interdiction would provoke a tempest. It seems, therefore, that empty shells have a mystical value, perhaps because they look like the natural counterparts of the coppers whose anatomical equivalents, according to the myths, are the scabs from sores themselves. More specifically, empty shells, scabs, and coppers, seem united by a double relationship: metaphorical, since the empty shells resemble the coppers, and the scabs are like a person's shells; and metonymical, insofar as the myths treat the shells and the scabs as a means of procuring the coppers.

8

The Origin of Copper

Supernatural beings equipped with a weepy baby or one that must be made to weep, or beings who themselves cry like small children, are very common in the Americas, and it can be assumed that they constitute a quite archaic theme since they have spread throughout the Western Hemisphere. The ancient Mexicans saw a malefic incarnation of the god Tlaloc in the otter—*auitzol* in Nahuatl—and lent it a cry similar to that of a weeping child; but woe unto the one who goes, full of compassion, in search of him: he will be captured and drowned. This belief is all the more interesting to me in as much as the Kwakiutl inverted the value attributed to otters by the Mexicans, from the negative to the positive. Indeed, they made sea otters the dispensers of great riches. Consequently, for them, the otters' function duplicates that of Lady Wealth. For their Tsimshian neighbors, it was an aquatic creature who presented her human sister-in-law with "a garment of wealth"; and, according to the Haida and the Tlingit, Lady Wealth enriches those who hear her baby cry.

Similar beliefs are found in South America. From the Guyanas to the Amazon, one hears of water spirits who cry like small children. One of these spirits appears in the shape of a marvelously beautiful woman who murders the boys she seduces. The Arawak of Guyana come even closer to the Indians of the North Pacific Coast, since they believe in a "Spirit of the Water" who, upon being surprised by a human, abandons her silver comb on the river bank.

The Tagish, who are contiguous to the Tlingit in the north and east, also knew a Lady Wealth whom they depicted in the form of a she-frog. Any man or woman who heard her child weeping and managed to capture it must refuse to give it back until the she-frog had excreted gold: further south, we have noticed this association of frogs with precious metals (p. 101). Indeed, according to the Kwakiutl, the frog can see what lies at the bottom of the water, and this natural aptitude allowed it to discover Komogwa's rich dwelling. As a reward, she received the privilege of cutting copper with her teeth. The Salish are even more distant from the Tagish, yet they echo them with their belief in a supernatural being that looks like a frog and cries like a baby. Whoever found it, enveloped it in a blanket, and kept it at home would surely become rich. This spirit (Komakwe) may be the same as the Kwakiutl marine god Komogwa, distributor of wealth. According to the Comox, Kōmōkoaē lives on the summit of a mountain in the shape of a grizzly bear. He has a great metal strongbox where he keeps his copper sheets, earrings, and other treasures. The Salish belief also reminds one of the Haida magic charm in the form of a stocky little personage. Its possession guaranteed an abundance of blankets and coppers to whoever stole it and stuffed it with pieces of valuable stolen objects.

The Tagish are Dene, members of the Athapaskan linguistic family, which, starting from roughly the 50th parallel, peopled the entire northwest of North America, but to the interior, behind the coastal tribes to which I have given my attention until now. Yet, the Dene too have myths about a Lady Wealth whose name was fittingly rendered by a French missionary of the latter half of the nineteenth century, Emile Petitot; he used the expression "La

Haida charm, dispenser of riches (from Swanton, Contributions to the Ethnology of the Haida)

femme aux métaux" or the "Mistress of Metals," which must be understood literally. Indeed, Indians attribute the discovery of copper to this no longer divine, but human, woman. On the other hand, while the Lady Wealth of the Tlingit and the Haida has a whimpering child, the Mistress of Metals has a voracious son (another way of showing insubordination) for an offspring.

The myth of the Mistress of Metals is known to us through numerous variants. Their general framework is the same, except on one point: sometimes the myth explains why copper has become difficult to extract; sometimes why the Europeans, and not the Indians, own the metals today. In both cases, therefore, the aim is to account for a loss, a relative loss in one case, an absolute loss in the other. But, everywhere, the heroine is a Dene woman whom an Eskimo hunter carried off, took far northward, and married. A son was born to them; the wife ran away with him one day. With an awl fixed to the tip of a stick, she succeeded in killing a caribou, which she cooked. The child threw himself on the meat with such voracity that the woman took fright and deserted him. She resumed her journey southward alone; she saw some bright lights on the way, which she took at first for camp-fires: it was the glare of an unknown substance from which, by beating it, she fashioned a knife for herself. The woman resumed her walk, arrived home, told the people about her discovery. She agreed to accompany the men to the copper on condition that they promise to respect her. But, when the men had manufactured all the metal tools they needed, they abused her. The woman refused to return home with them and, instead, sat on the mine. On their next trip, the men found her in the same place, but she had sunk up to her waist in the ground; the copper, too, was half buried. Again, she refused to accompany the men and ordered them to bring her back some meat on their next trip. When they returned, the woman and the copper had disappeared. The men left the meat there. A year later, they found her changed into copper that was too hard or too soft according to whether it came from the liver or the lungs. Other versions say only that the copper disappeared underground.

In another book, I put two images in opposition, that of the canoe and that of the floating island, proposing to see in them two moving bodies on the surface of the water, but one connoting culture and the other, nature. The myth of the Mistress of Metals confirms this interpretation. The fugitive woman perceives in the distance a herd of caribou, which she mistakes at first for a floating island; and, in at least one version, every night, with a pole driven in the mud, the woman moors the vessel in which she is escaping. She bivouacs on the shallow sea, and her immobile boat becomes her house. Nothing could better indicate (and even do so twice) that, breaking a conjugal bond, the woman's flight is the opposite of a canoe trip even though it too is made by water. As a matter of fact, in other American myths, the canoe trip symbolizes the quest for a wife at a good distance away, as opposed to the woman carried off by an Eskimo in the present myth, whose marriage took place "very far away, on the other side of the sea of ice," thus at too great a distance for it to have a chance to last. This too-distant union, to an enemy and under duress, is in contrast with the equally immoderate behavior—though in the opposite direction— of the heroine's kin, who commit at least social incest by raping her, a mistake that causes either the loss of the copper or its extraction to become difficult from then on.

This reading of the Dene myth in terms of a sociological code is corroborated by the symmetrical Tlingit myth. An incestuous brother and sister had to part. The brother became the Thunderbird who is responsible for hurricanes and tempests. Once a year, in the stormy season, he comes back to visit his sister. The latter, named Agischanak in the old sources, Hayicanak in more recent ones, went underground at the top of a mountain. Since then, she has supported the column on which the earth rests; she likes humans who make a fire to warm her, because each time she gets hungry, the ground shakes and the humans burn grease to feed her. According to other versions, the quakes occur when she fights off Raven, the trickster, who, to destroy men, jostles her and tries to make her lose her grip on the column supporting the earth. If this myth on the origin of earthquakes is in symmetrical relation to the Dene myth, it must follow from this that the movement by which the heroine of this latter myth digs herself into the ground with the copper is an inverted earthquake: in one case the earth opens itself up, in the other, it closes in on itself. I shall return to this point.

For the moment, two other details will hold my attention. In the recent versions of the Tlingit myth, the brother and sister guilty of a too-close union are the offspring of a marriage between a woman and a dog, that is to say, of a too-distant union, which reestablishes the framework of the Dene and other myths I have already examined. Furthermore, before making his mistake, the incestuous young man performs many meritorious acts. Notably, with the help of his brothers, he steals from the great bear a dangerous "shiny ring with a sharp edge." Broken in two pieces and thrown in the sky, this ring later becomes the rainbow.

We meet this hoop again further south among the Salish, first in a myth of the Squamish group, which concerns the origin of copper. Through the intermediary of the Tlingit version, therefore, this myth brings me back to the Dene myth devoted to the same theme. Two brothers had six sons each. The youngest son of one of the brothers was afflicted with a large protuberance on one side of his stomach. One day the twelve boys saw a man on the top of a mountain. He was rolling down the slope a big copper ring, which glinted and shone in the sunlight, and he made it come back to him by drawing in his breath. The twelve succeeded in stealing the ring, and passed it from hand to hand among themselves; but the owner, a wizard, gave chase and killed them off one after another, except for the deformed one who threw his stomach lump at his adversary: a dense fog arose, thanks to which he escaped. Desperate because of the death of their children, his father and uncle jumped into the flames of a fire. Their eyes flew out like sparks, the right eyes went north, the left ones, south. Immediately the fog lifted. After giving way to this show of mourning, the survivor's uncle undertook to hammer the ring, which he made into a copper cloth. Thus protected and armed with wild sheep horns, he killed his sons' murderer, retrieved their undamaged hearts from the wizard's stomach, put them back in place, and resurrected the boys. The uncle then molded the copper cloth into the figure of a boy to whom he gave the breath of life. The boy grew into a powerful man. Made of copper, he was invulnerable and became a mighty chief and a great huntsman.

A Kwakiutl belief throws light on the protuberant stomach theme. According to these Indians, if you touch a toad, it will settle in your stomach. You will become afflicted with an insatiable hunger, your skin will turn green like the toad's and your eyes will bulge. You will go from house to house, begging for food. The toad will grow large in your stomach; it will swell and you will die. Greedy children are said to be like people who have a toad in their stomach.

This is a valuable comment, because it allows me to connect the voracious child of the Dene myth with the young Salish hero endowed with a protuberant stomach. It undoubtedly is the same character, whose value, however, is inverted from one group to the other. Much further south, the Wasco (who are Chinook of the lower Columbia) speak in their myths of a weepy child, only one year old, who knows the past and can predict the future, and whose big stomach is sonorous like a bell when it is struck. One day, the mother suggested to another son that he step on his young brother's stomach to make it smaller; snakes, lizards, and frogs came out of it. Later, the two boys killed the sun whose heat was unbearable to humans. The eldest took the place of the sun and the younger one became the moon. Ever since then, the sun was less hot and the heavenly bodies alternated regularly in the sky.

Clearly, these myths translate into terms of a cosmological code the problem of "setting up a good distance," which was formulated in sociological terms by those I was examining earlier. Like the brother and sister who part forever in the Tsimshian myth (p. 97), the eyes of the two fathers in the Salish myth (now changed, one could say, into stars) split to the north and south. The Chinook boy with the big stomach that rings metallically becomes the moon and his brother, the sun, keeping a good distance between each other and a good distance from the earth, too. Again, the Thompson, who are inland Salish, make a character dressed in copper—who is singularly like the one in the myth of their Squamish neighbors—the son of the sun; for this reason, they call a beetle of a bright bronze color "son of the sun."

I have just mentioned the Thompson. These Indians share with their Shuswap neighbors a myth very much like that of the Squamish, except that the sons of the two men—who are called Coyote and Antelope (*Antilocapra*)—steal, not a copper hoop, but a glittering ball of gold or copper (according to the versions) filled with excrement. Coyote seizes the ball brought back by Antelope's only surviving son (all his own sons being dead) and changes himself into an elk whose body is covered by the armor-like metallic envelope of the ball. He confronts the murderer of his sons and nephews, but is killed in combat because one spot on his body has remained vulnerable. Other versions say that the children of Coyote and Antelope married each other; these mixed unions were the reason for the different colorings in skin and hair we see among Indians today. Elsewhere, these differences are explained by Coyote's marriage to two women with red and white skin, respectively; or else, again, the myths account for the present distance between the two animal families that gave their names to the heroes' fathers. Thus, here the code changes from cosmological or sociological to anatomical or zoological; but the problem remains the same: how to arbitrate between distinctive features.

Let me stop a moment with the cosmological code and see it take a new turn. The inland Salish have this explanation for the existence of the rainbow or the sun: in the beginning, a copper ring was stolen by a boy who is either lame (and thus afflicted with a periodically abnormal gait) or dirty and covered with sores, who, of course, reminds us of the hero in the Swaihwé origin myth (chap. 2). A version of the Skokomish group specifies that, at one time, the shining hoop was the plaything of the rich, while the poor had nothing with which to amuse themselves. The theft of the hoop put an end to this injustice. Whether the copper ring becomes the sun (Cowlitz version) or whether its theft is the incidental cause of the appearance of the rainbow, as the Skokomish say, from now on, these heavenly bodies will shine for everybody, without distinction of social rank or wealth.

By returning with these myths to the Salish, with whom I started this book, we have come full circle. But this is also true in another sense: in the Skokomish myth, the copper, democratized so to speak, rises into the sky, from which, according to the island Salish, it had first come down in aristocratic form: as the Swaihwé mask, privilege of a few noble lineages who, through it, hold the magic means of becoming rich. True, the Swaihwé mask is not the copper, but it does make possible its acquisition. Handed down by hereditary right or through marriage, this means of getting rich remains in the hands of the privileged, who extract rent from those who wish to use it. This proves that, in the groups where the mask exists, the mythical representations pertaining to it remain subordinated to the socio-economic infrastructure: they could not claim to create it if they did not first reflect it.

It is therefore significant that the myths hypostasizing copper in the shape of heavenly bodies came from the Salish groups whose social organization was no more egalitarian, it is true, than that of their neighbors who did not have the mask. Deprived of this method of sanctioning and perpetuating inequality through a magical and ritual instrument, they could treat themselves, at lesser cost, to the luxury of an ideology that, in a metaphorical way it is true (because the rainbow and the sun, which shine in the sky *like* copper, in this context have only a metaphorical value), concedes the enjoyment of copper to the greatest number of people. In fact, this enjoyment promised by the myths is an illusion, since it concerns celestial bodies which dispense their spectacle and benefactions to all men, and since the myths add only a symbolic value to these gratuitous advantages: the symbol of material riches, which, in real life, are only parsimoniously allotted to the humblest.

9

Coppers, Women, and Frogs

The Dene myth which I have just analyzed recounts how the Indians first obtained copper, in the concrete form of pieces found in rough state on the surface of the ground. To obtain copper, it had been necessary for a woman ravished by an Eskimo enemy to break up the exogamous but too greatly distanced union that he had imposed on her, and then, leaving her husband to journey to her own family, to reveal to them the existence of the copper found along the way:

(Escape and return of the heroine, bringing back the copper to her own people)

This journey inverts the one by which the Kwakiutl want to bring about the transfer of the woman and coppers to the in-laws, except that these coppers are not pieces of native metal, but are richly decorated objects whose function is equivalent to that of the Swaihwé masks among the Salish. In fact, the masks and the coppers circulate in the same direction:

The Dene myth, therefore, describes the opposite of a Salish-style marriage or of a marriage potlatch such as the Kwakiutl used to hold. But there is more to it. The Dene myth ends with the loss of the copper, consequent upon the incest of which the heroine's kin became guilty when they abused her. It also contradicts the Coast Salish origin myth of the Swaihwé, where a brother and sister who are dangerously close (as are the Dene heroine and her "brothers" when she agrees to travel alone with them; she is so well aware of her danger that, before leaving, she requests a promise that she will be respected by them) get out of this almost incestuous situation by obtaining the Swaihwé masks: the instruments of exogamous marriage, say the myths, but which also put an end to an improper intimacy. Thus, if the copper is taken away from the Dene as punishment for incest, the Swaihwé mask is given to the Salish as a means of avoiding it.

This being the case, it is important to note that the Salish groups practiced a systematic exogamy among themselves, with the principal aim, say the observers, of guaranteeing through these marriages the safety of their people in foreign countries. Exogamous marriage protects like armor. We can understand better now that the Squamish—whose origin myth of the Swaihwé, as I have noted, is equivocal and helps them mainly to base the friendly relations they maintain with their neighbors on a tradition of common origin (see p. 33)—stand also mid-way between the groups who say the Swaihwé came down from the sky and those who, on the contrary, make the copper rise up to heaven where it becomes a celestial body or phenomenon. As a matter of fact, their myth of the copper's origin unfolds entirely on earth from which copper comes and where it stays, first in the shape of an armor that gives invulnerability to its wearer, then in the shape of a hero with a copper body endowed with the same quality.

The Swaihwé mask—means to an exogamous marriage, that is, the transformation of real or virtual enemies into affines—accordingly appears in the Salish myths as that which brings off the most improbable of consents. Under the name Xwéxwé, the Kwakiutl own the Swaihwé, which they have borrowed from the Salish, but they invert its function and transfer it to the copper. This function of the copper, analogous to that of the Swaihwé, extends further north to the Tlingit, who do not seem to have owned the mask. Their version of a myth, very widespread elsewhere, sheds a particularly good light on this function.

A princess one day stepped on the dung of a grizzly bear. She hurled insults in the animal's direction; the latter appeared immediately under human guise and carried her off. She succeeded in escaping (pp. 95, 102), however, and found a magic boat that took her to the sun. The sun's sons fell in love with her, but they were already married. They therefore first killed their wife, a cannibal, and they scattered her chopped-up body. The pieces came down in Tsimshian country where, ever since then, cannibals abound. The heroine took her solar husbands, and the son she had had by them, back to her village: they were well received, but she allowed a fellow countryman to woo her, and her husbands left her. From the sky to which they had returned, they vowed to give her and the child a miserable lot. The two lived, isolated and scorned, in a poor house on top of which people kept throwing the leavings of food. For this reason, the son was nicknamed Garbage-Man. One day, he discovered his father's solid copper boat, cut it up in pieces, and with them built a house of copper that was hidden under branches. All day long, he pounded the copper and filled his dwelling with treasures. It must be said that, in those days, there was no iron or copper.

A young girl of marriageable age lived in the village, but her parents refused all her suitors. Our hero managed to seduce her by having her sniff a roll of copper while asleep. She followed him as far as his home, was stunned by the solid copper door, and agreed to marry him. They looked for her everywhere and finally found her in the house, which, once rid of its camouflage of branches, shone with such brilliance that those who came near it had to take a step back. Metallic gifts softened the young lady's father, and it is since that time that Indians have owned copper.

Entered into by way of the copper, this marriage thus united spouses who are twice removed: he is celestial, she terrestrial; and one would have feared that their diametrically opposed social conditions would forever have rendered impossible a union all the more problematical because all of the suitors had been rejected so far. But, emphasizes the myth, the power of the copper forces consent. And it derives power above all from the fact that it shines so strongly that it cannot be looked at in the face: like the sun, whose son Garbage-Man is.

One detects a secret cause of this power: extracted from the depths of the earth, or, drawn from the bottom of the waters, as some myths also say, the copper represents a chthonian sun. Through its luminous aspect and its dark origin, the copper brings about a marriage of opposites, which is what all marriages are in social systems characterized, as they are on the Pacific Coast, by a permanent state of tension between lineages, and where only marriage at a good distance manages to arbitrate between the contradictory principles of exogamy and endogamy.

Consequently, and if, as all this work shows, the Swaihwé masks are interchangeable with the copper, several peculiarities of their appearance are explained. The Swaihwé masks have a "nose" and are fitted with "horns" in the shape of bird heads. They are trimmed with feathers, and feathers dominate the dancers' costume, too. In fact, the island Salish say that they came down from the sky. But, through their aquatic origin, according to the mainland Salish myths, which say they were fished from the bottom of a lake, and through their lolling tongue—an organ which other myths liken to a fish—they too achieve a marriage of opposites: they pertain both to air and to water. One can include them therefore in that vast family of mediators, such as the plumed serpent of the ancient Aztecs, whose function is expressed by an assemblage of normally incompatible terms: the sky and the chthonian world, or, again, the sky and water.

The frog fulfills the same function, but for a different reason: instead of embodying extreme and contradictory terms, it stands midway between the earth and the water. One remembers the role assigned to this animal by the myths. In the Fraser myths, the hero, a potential suicide, kills himself when the salmon he has just caught turns into a frog; or, conversely, he is dissuaded from taking this fatal step when the disease abandons him in the form of frogs (p. 27). The hero in a Kwakiutl myth, sick also, owes his cure to a she-toad, who rubs him with a medicine drawn from her nest and presents him with a precious piece of copper (p. 37).

Lady Wealth of the Haida avenges a martyred frog, which is probably none other than herself; whereas, among the Tlingit, the same divinity tortures with her copper fingernails those whom she will later enrich by way of the wounds she has inflicted on them (p. 106). According to the Kwakiutl, gluttons have a toad in their stomach (pp. 112–13), a belief that the Tsimshian invert by making a hero (who is not greedy but prodigal with food) become the content of a frog, instead of its container.

Let me stop for a moment on this myth. A despised orphan, nephew of the village chief, succeeds, single-handedly, in seizing a lump of copper that had fallen from the sky like a fiery meteor and remained suspended on top of a tree. The chief had promised his daughter to whoever would accomplish this great feat, but, much ashamed that the girl had been won by his nephew, he abandoned them both and moved away, taking the whole village population with him, except the girl's grandmother who decided to stay with her. The poor little boy was too young yet to provide for the needs of three people. Their situation grew worse. One

Kwakiutl frog mask with copper teeth (University of British Columbia Museum of Anthropology)

day, he saw coming out of a lake a great frog whose claws, mouth, eyes, and eyebrows were made of copper. He caught it in a trap by causing the two halves of a split tree to close in on it. The poor little boy killed the frog and clothed himself in its skin. Henceforth, he caught quantities of salmon and even killed whales. At the same time, he became a handsome youth with very clean skin, instead of the sickly boy he had been before. They lived in plenty, and welcomed the famished villagers when the latter begged for their help. The hero forgave his uncle, who was now his father-in-law. Time passed. The hero continued to bring back to the village enormous supplies of fish and game, but, upon returning from his expeditions, he found it increasingly difficult to remove his frog skin. Finally, he gave up and told his wife that he would from now on live at the bottom of the seas, from which he would send her, and her family, too, the food they needed. They would find all their necessities on the beach: seals, halibut, whales, porpoises. The village never lacked anything, but it never saw its benefactor again.

The Tlingit, who have almost the same myth, specify that the generous monster, into which the hero transforms himself, is none other than Gonaqadet whose affinity to Komogwa I have already stressed (p. 105). Komogwa, the Kwakiutl sea god and master of riches, is always described as a corpulent personage; similarly, the corpulence of the mythical batrachian (or else the corpulence it causes) is always pointed out. Between poverty and wealth, between famine and abundance, and also between spouses who are too distant, the frog therefore accomplishes, in its own way (which is that of a middle term), the same mediation that among the Salish the Swaihwé masks (which unite extreme terms) are charged with producing. The place occupied by the frog or the toad in a vast mythological system is thus explained.

10

Earthquakes and Cylinder Eyes

The investigation I have been pursuing since the beginning of this work has yielded two important results. We already knew that the same myths often invert themselves when passing from one population to another, and it will be useful at this point, in order to refresh our memory, to give a few examples involving characters who have become familiar to us.

The Kwakiutl's Komogwa lives at the bottom of the waters and rids a lost Indian woman of the beard afflicting her (chap. 7). By contrast, his Salish equivalent Kōmōkoaē lives at the top of a mountain (chap. 8) and gives back to a bald-headed, lost Indian woman the locks that had been torn off her. (The Kwakiutl themselves seem aware of this transformation and sometimes describe Komogwa as a "mountain spirit" instead of master of the ocean.) Similarly, the Kwakiutl and the Salish know Cannibal-at-the-north-end-of-the-world, Baxbakwalanuxsiwaé, but the Kwakiutl make him a chief who resides deep in the woods, and the Salish have him a slave who lives in the outer confines of the ocean. Finally, while the Salish ogress Tal corresponds to the Dzonokwa of the Kwakiutl (p. 66), the latter has a habit of blinding the children she steals by gluing their eyes with gum, whereas Tal, blind instead of blinding, suffers the same lot in the hands of the children

Komogwa (courtesy of American Museum of Natural History, no. 2A11283)

she has taken away. As for the Swaihwé mask, another striking example can be found in chapter 12.

Furthermore, I have noted that the plastic features of masks carrying the same message are inverted in exactly the same fashion when they pass from one population to its neighbor. Such is, in fact, the relationship we find between the Swaihwé mask, the Salish dispenser of riches, and the mask of Dzonokwa whose mythic and ritual role is the same for the Kwakiutl. Conversely, when the plastic elements remain unchanged, as between the Salish Swaihwé mask and its Kwakiutl imitation under the name of Xwéxwé, it is the messages that are then inverted (p. 92). This remarkable phenomenon may be illustrated by a diagram, in which the solid lines represent the plastic form and the dotted lines the message:

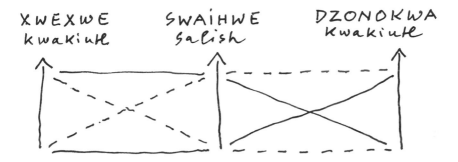

Secondly, the same relationship of inversion already noted between the respective Salish and Kwakiutl masks also prevails on the mythic level between the Dene, on the one hand, and several coast tribes on the other: the Kwakiutl and certain of their neighbors, including all the Salish. In fact, the Dene assign to copper a function opposite to that given it by the Kwakiutl, and to that given by the Salish to the Swaihwé mask, which, as we have shown, is interchangeable for copper when viewed from this angle.

To bring my double demonstration to a conclusion, one last aspect of the problem remains to be dealt with because, for the

Kwakiutl, the Xwéxwé mask and the Dzonokwa are opposed to each other in still another way. Intimately associated with earthquakes, which they are alleged to provoke, the Xwéxwé masks make the floor boards of the house shake when they dance. On her part, the Dzonokwa makes the roof shake (pp. 71, 73). We have also noticed the link between earthquakes and the Swaihwé masks among the Salish (pp. 20, 40–41).

In imagination, at least, earthquakes can have an interesting result: one can hope that by opening itself, the earth will expose the metallic wealth it hides. Doubtless this is a theoretical result, with scant chance of verification in the facts; but it is striking that the Dene myths illustrate it with its opposite: by closing in on itself again, the earth conceals its metallic riches from men, instead of opening itself up to reveal them. The Dene myths, therefore, are not content with reversing the direction in which the copper flows in matrimonial exchanges, in a way that contradicts Kwakiutl practice. They also invert the notion of earthquakes, which the Salish associate with these exchanges and which the Kwakiutl continue to associate with the same masks—Salish instruments of matrimonial alliance—but which they turn into misers, thus the opposite of generous donors.

Consequently, among the Salish, the Swaihwé masks simultaneously connote easily acquired riches, earthquakes, and marriage at good distance (chap. 2), which is the opposite of incest. The Xwéxwé masks of the Kwakiutl also connote marriage at a good distance, which is the occasion for their transmission, and earthquakes, which their dancers know how to provoke. But their relationship with wealth is the opposite of that prevailing between the latter and the Swaihwé masks, because the Xwéxwé refuse or even withdraw it instead of dispensing it. The Tlingit, who do not have the mask, link incest to the origin of earthquakes (p. 111), a relationship which the Dene invert by making of the contrary of an earthquake (and of the loss of the greatest wealth, copper) the consequence of an incest, and not its cause. This new slant confirms the practical value of the complex system of transformations which I have unravelled. At the same time, I am led to point out some curious analogies between the mythology of earthquakes in ancient Japan (traces of which subsist to this day) and in the American Northwest, a connection that might seem far-fetched if prehistoric finds made in the latter region were not singularly reminiscent of others from northern Japan. The existence of a common base of archaic beliefs cannot, therefore, *a priori* be ruled out.

This is not the only analogy. Some Chinese tombs from the end of the Chou dynasty have yielded sculpted wooden effigies, which, with their lolling tongue and protuberant eyes, look strikingly like the Swaihwé masks. Whether or not a common descent may be traced linking these sculptures and others with dangling tongue from Indonesia and New Zealand is a much debated question that

Archaic Chinese wooden figure with protuberant eyes and lolling tongue, Chou dynasty (from Salmony, Antler and Tongue)

remains controversial. But it does not directly affect the problem I wish to raise, except, perhaps, in this, that the Japanese attributed earthquakes to certain fish of the Siluridae family of catfish, which they liked to represent with protuberant eyes. More important still is the fact that this link between fish and earthquakes is accompanied by others I have already noted in America. In Japan, too, earthquakes afford the opportunity to acquire metallic riches, which are identified with dejecta, just as they are by the coast people (pp. 102, 114) and the Dene: the latter call copper by a name which means excrement of bear or beaver. Finally, Dr. C. Ouwehand, from whom I have borrowed several of the preceding data, shows that in ancient Japanese thought seisms play the part of righters of social and economic inequalities, a function, as we have seen (pp. 114–15), that the Salish assigned to copper, which is itself linked to earth tremors and which, in this part of America, in fact acts as mediator (the agent of exogamous marriage) between fellow-citizens and strangers.

As for the silurids, they occupied a not-insignificant place in the mythology of this region of the New World. From the Shuswap to the Coeur d'Alene, the inland Salish know a myth about a great culture hero, son of an Indian woman and the edible root of hog-fennel (*Peucedanum macrocarpum*), an umbellifer to which the people of the sea coast, on their part, attribute magic power. Chewed and then spat out, the root disperses the wind and tempests, and the seeds, treated likewise, ward off sea monsters. It is said of the Child of the Root that he transformed into a catfish a father who had laughed at him because of his origin. Later, he became the moon. But, the hero to whom the inland Salish give the same destiny has a mother and a grandmother who are associated with quakes and swamps (the habitat of the Siluridae?), respectively. Since these Salish invert into celestial exogamy the vegetable and chthonian exogamy from which the hero of the first myth has sprung—unless they make him a virgin's son by neutralizing the exogamous relationship instead of inverting it—one may ask if the father-turned-catfish of the inland myths, who tries to cast away the hero, does not represent a symmetrical counterpart of the hero's mother (sometimes the grandmother), who is called Earthquake and who, after her son has been carried off, by contrast, attempts to retrieve him.

Let me close this parenthesis, for it is not my intention to extend to Japan and China an investigation that, on the contrary, draws its strength from the fact that it has been restricted to one region of North America. It is, undoubtedly, a vast region, but I have observed several times that the people who inhabit it maintained very close contacts among themselves, evidenced either by a common language (this is the case of the Salish as a whole) or by migrations, wars, borrowings, commercial and matrimonial exchanges, of which archeology, traditional legends, and history supply the proofs. This ecumene extended from Alaska in the north down to the lower valley of the Columbia River in the south. I have underlined the symmetrical relationships prevailing between the Dene myths and those of their coast neighbors. But it is on the coast itself, from the Tlingit to the Chinook, that this symmetry is most clearly brought out.

It will be remembered that the Tlingit link the resplendent glare of copper to its celestial origin: the first copper known to man came from a boat made entirely of this metal that belonged to the sons of the sun (p. 118). According to these same Indians, in the beginning of time, when darkness still reigned on earth, all the animal species were blended. A myth relates that a demiurge stole and opened a receptacle where the sun was locked up. Immediately, "it shone in all its splendor in the sky. At the sight of it, the people (that is, as yet undifferentiated primitive living beings) dispersed in all directions; some to the forests where they became the quadrupeds, others to the trees where they became the

birds, others finally to the water where they became the fish."
But, at the other end of the area I have chosen to consider, the
Chinook invert this system, which they also translate into aquatic
instead of celestial terms. One of the tribes in this family, the
Kathlamet, say that the first copper floated on the surface of the
water where it shone like the sun. All the men of the village tried
to shoot it with arrows to catch it, but the thing always escaped
them. Only the chief's two daughters, disguised as men, succeeded.* They brought back the copper in their canoe; it was cut
into pieces, which were distributed among the inhabitants. The
birds received the "blood" as their share; all had a little bit of red
to put on the head, and were painted green, white, or black on
the rest of the body. Blue-Jay got the most beautiful colors, but
Clam stole them and jumped with them to the bottom of the
water; and ever since then, Clam has the mother-of-pearl colors.

   Thus, like the Tlingit, the Chinook trace the distinctions between species back to the first appearance of copper, with this sole
difference, that for the former the sun was master of the copper,
whereas the latter have a first copper without master that shines
like the sun. As is often observed at the conclusion of a series of
mythic transformations, whenever one transformation affects the
content, another is added which inverts the form. For the Tlingit,
the relationship of the copper with the sun is of a metonymical
order: it proceeds from it. Among the Kathlamet (and though, for
them, the copper comes from the water), this relationship subsists
on the rhetorical plane, but it is changed into metaphor: "It was
shining like the sun. . . . When it turned one way it looked
red; then it looked green, then white . . . it was just like the
sun."

---

   *Compare this travesty with the belief, attested by the coastal people, from
the Columbia estuary in the south up to the Yukon much further north, that
"the Sun and other beings specially associated with metal are 'half-men.' "

If this dazzling brilliance of the copper constitutes the invariant trait of the system, one can better understand the last reason for the opposition that, on the plastic level, prevails between the Swaihwé masks and Dzonokwa. Dzonokwa's eyes are deeply sunk in their orbits, or are half-closed, because they are forever dazzled. The Swaihwé, on the contrary, has bulging eyes; this anatomical peculiarity must mean that they cannot be dazzled. Now, among other riches that these two supernatural beings procure for humans is copper, but the transfer is not made in the same way. The Dzonokwa has it taken from her, often at the cost of her life; generous, the Swaihwé guarantees its acquisition.

That the cylindrical eyes of the Swaihwé denote an imperturbable vision is an interpretation which, of course, needs to be corroborated. It does seem as though, throughout North America, myths and rites assign to the cylinder a role consisting in capturing, fixing, and putting into direct communication terms that are very far apart. Along the whole Pacific north coast, the shamans have "soul catchers": small ivory or carved-wood objects, often of tubular shape, used to catch and imprison the fugitive soul of a sick person in order to reincorporate it. According to the Tlingit myths, Raven, the trickster, before leaving the Indians, had warned them that upon his return to earth, no one would be able to look at him with the naked eye without being turned to stone. Henceforward, one would have to espy him through a tube made of a rolled-up leaf of skunk cabbage. Thus, when La Pérouse's vessels were driven ashore in 1786, the neighboring Tlingit thought that these great birds, whose wings were the sails, were none other than Raven and his retinue. They hastily made up their curious telescopes. Equipped with protuberant eyes, they believed that they had thus enhanced their visual power, and now dared to contemplate the astonishing spectacle that presented itself to their sight. The Eskimos of north Alaska, and, more to the east, the Copper

Kwakiutl Dzonokwa mask with half-closed eyes (Museum für Völkerkunde, Berlin)

Kwakiutl Xwéxwé mask (Milwaukee Public Museum of Milwaukee County)

Eskimos, both neighbors of the Dene, associate bulging eyes with a piercing vision, or they attribute them to the efforts involved when one tries to see in the dark. According to the Shuswap, who are inland Salish, the spirit of the wind (which is, as we say, "penetrating") has a large head and protruding eyes. The shamans of Algonkin-speaking tribes in eastern Canada have magic telescopes made of hollow juniper wood wrapped in white caribou skin. The "shaking tent," also white, in which they enclose themselves for their trances, is designed like a cylinder: an empty column permitting an infinite view, far above and below. A similar belief is found in South America among the Tucano of Vaupès.

Widespread in the New World, these representations take on an even more precise shape among the Menomini of the Great Lakes. They say that the sun stops on its run at midday in order to contemplate the earth through a long cylinder of copper. The hollow tubes of the Kiowa ritual pipes constitute a kind of reduced model of this cylinder. The archeological sites of North America have yielded, in abundance, small copper leaves rolled into cylinders, which may perhaps be related to this symbolic imagery.

That the bulging eyes of the Swaihwé are also derived from it is, in any case, borne out by the information already given about them. I have noted their immovable nature (p. 98). It will also be remembered that during the dances, a clown armed with a lance tries to put them out (see pp. 17, 26). He must be seeking in vain to blind the masks, whose eyes, on the contrary, attest by their peculiar shape that they are clairvoyant.

11

The Nature of a Style

The affinity to copper manifested by the Swaihwé masks translates itself in the fact that they are impervious to its dazzle: this is what, in short, their protuberant eyes mean. This observation allows me to solve the last problem, raised by the peculiar shape of the decorated copper objects which the Kwakiutl and their northern neighbors held as their most precious possessions. The most important of these coppers were given an identity expressed in a distinctive name. Toward the end of the nineteenth century, they could attain a value of several thousand (contemporary) dollars, and their owner enjoyed a corresponding amount of public credit. He could keep them, but, in general, they were destined to change hands in the course of potlatches, sold or given away whole or in fragments (see chap. 6). Sometimes the owner would even throw them into the sea, to prove his wealth by sacrificing such a treasure for his personal glory and that of his lineage.

In general, these coppers always have the same shape: curving at the apex and the base, with sides narrowing from the top to the middle part, then diverging slightly or staying parallel below. The upper portion is often very richly decorated with the image of the front view of an animal, or of its face. Almost rectangular and devoid of ornament, the lower portion, or "hindquarters,"

135

Figure of a Kwakiutl holding a copper (Museum für Völkerkunde, Berlin)

shows only two perpendicular ridges, beaten in relief and reminiscent of the "chief-pale" motif in the language of heraldic blazons: one horizontal, at the level where the slanting upper sides are at their closest, and the other vertical, from the "chief" to the base of the copper, which one could view as a kind of shield.

This complicated shape is all the more enigmatic since no specimen anterior to contact with whites is known. All the coppers that have been seen or collected are made of sheet metal of European origin, and it cannot be ascertained that, before its introduction here, these objects were manufactured from native copper and in what form. To an investigator who in 1920 interrogated the

Broken Kwakiutl copper (University of British Columbia Museum of Anthropology)

Tlingit, the latter replied that the shape represents Gonaqadet's forehead. The lower portion, then, must have corresponded to the frontal bone, and the upper portion to the effigy of a person or of a face adorning the monster's headdress. This interpretation is confirmed by a decorated monument, but Gonaqadet does not seem to have been represented always in this fashion. One cannot therefore generalize from a single example, and even if other examples were found, one would not be able to say if the shape of the coppers is derived from them or if, on the contrary, they are inspired by it. We shall see in chapter 14 that, when viewed from another angle, this interpretation is of very great interest.

Credit is due to Paul S. Wingert for having first noticed that a resemblance of a more general order exists between the outline of the coppers and that of the Swaihwé masks. Although the two objects spring from different cultures, their whole shape and the respective proportions of lower and upper parts are the same, and, in both cases, a ridge or vertical band runs across the middle of the lower part. Wingert, however, relegates his observation to a note and does nothing further to exploit it. The comparisons I have made in the present work allow me to pick it up again and give it a much wider significance. We know, of course, that even among the Salish, the Swaihwé masks are interchangeable with copper, since identical myths account for the origins of both (p. 35); and that, among the Kwakiutl, the origin of the coppers I have just described goes back to the Dzonokwa personage whose mask inverts the Swaihwé from the plastic point of view, whereas it maintains the same function from a semantic point of view. By contrast, it is the semantic function that is reversed when we pass from the Salish Swaihwé to the Kwakiutl Xwéxwé—but then, the plastic shape of the two masks remains unchanged.

Consequently, the deep cause of the resemblance noted by Wingert is clear. If the coppers have the same general look as the Swaihwé masks, it is because they parallel them among the Kwakiutl, both as sources of wealth and as a means to matrimonial alliance, which brings protection against endogamy and security against foreign peoples. The coppers and the masks constituted two parallel solutions to the same problems for two different but contiguous populations, connected by all sorts of commercial and matrimonial exchanges whenever wars did not otherwise bring them into contact.

To understand the origin of this parallelism, I am, it is true, reduced to hypotheses. But these may rest on a few solid foundations. The shape of the coppers would remain unexplainable if it did not derive from that of the Swaihwé masks. Yet, even taking into account the archaic style, which, in any case, they share with all the other products of Salish art, it does not seem that these masks spread on the coast and on Vancouver Island in very ancient times. Peoples without writing often condense their genealogies and their testimony remains subject to caution on this account. I will come back to this in Part II, but this is no reason to ignore the fact that the Musqueam trace back to only five generations the transfer of the mask from the coast to the islands. They themselves got it from groups established in the Fraser valley; beyond that, the first origin is lost.

Be that as it may, it is only after the mask reached the island (from which it re-crossed the strait to pass on to Salish groups further north) that the Nootka and the Kwakiutl could become acquainted with it and adopt it. Among the Kwakiutl, this borrowing would have been made in two ways, perhaps even in two stages: first from afar, and as an idea engendering the coppers, which fulfill the same social and economic functions. As a matter of fact, on the plastic level, the coppers retain only the abstract outline of the masks; but, in the substance of which they are made, they materialize the masks' conceptual essence—because, as we have seen, the Salish Swaihwé already connotes wealth, and hence

Kwakiutl chief holding a copper with protruding "eyes" (from Boas, Social Organization and Secret Societies of the Kwakiutl)

copper. A photograph published by Boas at the end of the last century shows a copper with, in the place where one usually sees a face, two protuberances which may be imitating the eyes of the Swaihwé.

Next, the Kwakiutl may have reconstructed in their fashion the mythology and ritual of the giant ogress who steals children, a theme they shared with all the coast peoples, from Alaska to the Columbia estuary and even further south. And as they had already caught the idea of the Swaihwé in the coppers, it had been taken out of commission, so to speak. They may, by contrast, have lent to the mask of Dzonokwa, this supernatural holder of the precious metal, the inverted plastic characteristics of the Swaihwé mask. Later on, or at the same time, on the occasion of intertribal marriages, the memory of which is preserved in traditional legends, the Southern Kwakiutl may have received the Swaihwé masks—but in flesh and bone this time, if one may say so—from their Comox neighbors. Supplanted in their original function by the coppers, placed in a new setting where they were superfluous, these masks may have been given the opposite function.

This historical reconstruction is plausible, but since the consequences it implies were already observable at the end of the nineteenth century, a recent diffusion of the Swaihwé would leave very little time for things to have happened that way. I would prefer to suppose either that the existence and diffusion of the Swaihwé mask go back to a more ancient period than the various local traditions suggest, or that, in the form in which they have come down to us, the coppers and the masks perpetuate, each in its own way and in more or less parallel fashion, archaic themes in whose search I will venture in chapter 14 (Part II).

Did these themes, from the start, rest on a figurative representation foreshadowing both the coppers and the Swaihwé? Nothing compels me to postulate this, because these emblems did not necessarily have a precursor. But, in order to complete my brief, it is perhaps fitting for me to take into account a third type of object, which is tied to the same system of representations as the other two.

In his early publications, Boas mentions certain objects which, concurrently with the coppers, held an important place in wedding ceremonies. They are the *gyī'serstâl* (*gyī'seqstâl, gisexstala*), wooden boards of very great age reminiscent of ceremonial box lids, but thicker, painted, and set with sea otter teeth. The wife's family sometimes amassed a considerable quantity of these objects, which they solemnly offered to the husband's family. Despite their

frequent decoration with eyes, each was supposed to represent a human lower jaw, a curious notion that Boas' informants did not always seem to interpret in the same way. For some, the *gisexstala* symbolized the right of the husband to command his wife to speak or to be silent, according to his wish; for others, the *gisexstala* represented the wife's teeth: if she did not give such boards to her husband, she was liable to be accused of carrying no teeth in her head, or of having teeth too weak to bite copper.

The Bella Coola share this second interpretation. Fifty years or so ago they still knew that, among their Kwakiutl neighbors, the woman offered her husband's family pieces of wood set with sea otter teeth: "This makes teeth for the bride." If she quarreled with another woman, she could draw back her lips and shame her rival by saying: "What can you do? You have no teeth, while I have two sets of them" (or as many sets as there were boards given at her marriage).

In passing from the *gisexstala,* through the intermediary of the copper, to the Swaihwé or Xwéxwé masks, it thus seems that a transfer was accomplished: in one case the teeth, in the other the eyes, appear to be the anatomical seat of a mysterious power. Such a transfer is all the more revealing perhaps, since, as we have seen, the lower jaw of the Swaihwé mask, sagging under the weight of an enormous tongue, is singularly lacking in bite . . .

Whatever the worth of this hypothesis, whose fragility I will not deny, it nonetheless remains that the coppers and the Swaihwé—to speak only of them—share the same spirit. For if among the Salish the Swaihwé is a means of obtaining wealth, I believe I have established that among the Kwakiutl the coppers— those supreme riches—are the metaphor for the Swaihwé, and this

A young Kwakiutl couple, the woman holding a gisexstala *surmounted with coppers (National Museums of Canada, no. 56909)*

rhetorical transformation brings me back to the literal sense from which I started.

It would be misleading to imagine, therefore, as so many ethnologists and art historians still do today, that a mask and, more generally, a sculpture or a painting may be interpreted each for itself, according to what it represents or to the aesthetic or ritual use for which it is destined. We have seen that, on the contrary, a mask does not exist in isolation; it supposes other real or potential masks always by its side, masks that might have been chosen in its stead and substituted for it. In discussing a particular problem, I hope to have shown that a mask is not primarily what it represents but what it transforms, that is to say, what it chooses *not* to represent. Like a myth, a mask denies as much as it affirms. It is not made solely of what it says or thinks it is saying, but of what it excludes.

Is not this the case for any work of art? Reflecting upon a few types of American tribal masks, I was led to raise a much vaster problem, that of style. Contemporary styles do not ignore one another. Even among peoples called primitive, a certain familiarity is established in the course of wars followed by pillage, intertribal ceremonies, marriages, markets, occasional commercial exchanges. The originality of each style, therefore, does not preclude borrowings: it stems from a conscious or unconscious wish to declare itself different, to choose from among all the possibilities some that the art of neighboring peoples has rejected. This is also true of successive styles. The Louis XV style prolongs the Louis XIV style, and the Louis XVI style prolongs the Louis XV style; but, at the same time, each challenges the other. In its own way, it says what the preceding style was saying in its own language, and it also says something else, which the preceding style was not saying but was silently inviting the new style to enunciate.

One of the most pernicious notions bequeathed us by functionalism, and which still keeps so many ethnologists under its rule, is that of isolated tribes, enclosed within themselves, each living on its own account a peculiar experience of an aesthetic, mythical, or ritual order. Thus, it is not recognized that before the colonial era and the centuries of destructive action—which, even in the most protected regions, the western world has exercised through its pathogenic germs and export products—these populations, being more numerous, were also elbow to elbow. With few exceptions, nothing that happened in one was unknown to its neighbors, and the modalities according to which each explained and represented the universe to itself were elaborated in an unceasing and vigorous dialogue.

To those who contest my right to interpret a population's myths or works of art by comparing them to the myths and works of art of other populations, and who deem legitimate only the method that consists in relating, say, a group's myths to its own social organization, its economic life, and religious beliefs, I will reply: of course, we must start there, and ask first from the ethnography of the group in question all it can yield. This is, as a matter of fact, what I have done ceaselessly in my research on American mythology, taking care for every group to surround myself with all the data of this kind gathered by myself and others in the field, or available in the literature. The literature provides the only data that can be used in the case of groups that have disappeared physically, or whose culture has collapsed in the course of the years, victims of a fate that could not justify this other crime, this time of a scientific order, which consists in behaving as if they had not existed. Only those whose entire ethnological outlook is confined to the group they have studied personally are prone to overlook my almost maniacal deference for the facts; as if, even today, the most fruitful and original work were not being carried on in Greek, Latin, or Hindu literature, which is several millennia old, on the legacies of people even more irrevocably gone than those I am being reproved for studying through their works without journeying to them. In three quarters of the cases, if not more, the journey would be futile in this kind of investigation, given the ruinous condition to which the irruption of the machine age has brought them . . .

That is not the real problem. Even assuming the best conditions—that is, a still-living culture, with well preserved beliefs and practices—the study of the internal correlations between its mythology or art and all the rest would constitute an absolutely necessary preliminary, but it would not be sufficient. Once these local resources have been tapped, further efforts are required of the analyst. For these myths are in opposition to other myths which they contradict or transform, and it would be impossible to understand one without reference to the others—in the same way that any utterance is explained with words which do not precisely figure in it, since those used by the speaker derive their meaning and importance from the fact that they were chosen in preference to others that he might have used, and to which, in commenting on the utterance, it is therefore quite in order to refer.

The importance of these explicit or implicit counterpoints is particularly well brought out in the cases examined in the present work. The plastic characteristics of the Dzonokwa masks remained unintelligible until I compared them to those of the Swaihwé masks. But, they come from populations with different languages and cultures, which were, nevertheless, near enough to each other for one of the two masks to have been borrowed. The plastic characteristics of the Xwéxwé mask, which belongs to the Kwakiutl, can only be explained as an imitation of the Salish Swaihwé mask. But its semantic load is a function of the one carried both by their Dzonokwa mask and by the Swaihwé among the Salish. Parallel or opposed, all these semantic functions form among themselves a system that originates in the ideology of copper, through whose intermediary alone light can be shed on the resemblances found, on the plastic level, between the Swaihwé masks of one group and the decorated coppers of the other.

In its turn, this ideology of copper and the social and economic functions it expresses require, in order to be understood, that we articulate the myths of the coast people with those of their inland neighbors, the Dene. Geographic proximity alone would legitimate the comparison, which draws additional justification from the fact that, in the American Northwest, the major copper deposits are in Athapaskan country and that, through the intermediary of the Tlingit, practically all the native copper came from there. That is not all: the Dene, or Northern Athapaskan, who in the past knew how to temper, anneal, and forge native copper, surpassed all their neighbors in the art of metallurgy. Perhaps, therefore, we should see in them the last heirs to that Old Copper Culture which flourished from the fifth millennium in the Great Lakes region and whose first representatives, as a consequence of climatic changes occurring around the third millennium, migrated north in the wake of the retreating arctic forest and its fauna, which made up their habitual game.

By means of logical operations that project at a distance, and transform or invert art objects, a story, which unfolded in the extreme north on a time scale of millennia, has come to overlap another more recent story with a shorter periodicity. This story, far to the south, attests to the Salish migrations from the mainland to the island, then from the island to the mainland, as well as the conflicts and alliances of these same Salish with the Southern Kwakiutl: developments whose memory is preserved in local traditions, even though they are transfigured into mythical events. Along a stretch of nearly three thousand kilometers, ideological structures were built up compatible with the inherent constraints of their mental nature and which, in agreement with these constraints, encoded, as we say today, the givens of the environment and of history. These ideological structures incorporate the information with pre-existing paradigms and also generate new ones in the shape of mythic beliefs, ritual practices, and plastic works. Over this immense territory, these beliefs, practices, and works remain mutually congruent when they imitate one another, and even, perhaps above all, when they seem to be contradictory. For in both cases they equilibrate each other beyond the linguistic, cultural, and political frontiers whose transparency was proved by my whole argument, unless their always relative closure sets up a logical as well as historical constraint and marks the points at which the inversions take place.

When he claims to be solitary, the artist lulls himself in a perhaps fruitful illusion, but the privilege he grants himself is not real. When he thinks he is expressing himself spontaneously, creating an original work, he is answering other past or present, actual or potential, creators. Whether one knows it or not, one never walks alone along the path of creativity.

Part II

12

*Beyond the Swaihwé**

The practitioner of structural analysis is almost always asked the same question: how are myth transformations brought about in real life? You line up myths which, from one population to another, contradict and invert each other or which show relationships of symmetry among themselves along several axes. This makes an impressive picture, but to be convinced, one would also want to understand how these abstract relations generate each other. In what historical or local circumstances, under what internal or external influences, in answer to what psychological motivations do these inversions originate in the mind of narrators and listeners who, in every other respect, function (one must suppose) in a more banal fashion? In sum, one refuses to ratify a whole system of completed structures springing forth, fully equipped, from the collective mind. Because, my critics say, this collective mind is nothing but a fiction behind which a multitude of individual minds stir: your structures resulted from certain procedures inside each of these minds, and it is these empirical processes that should be

*Originally titled "Histoire d'une structure," in W. E. A. van Beek and J. H. Scherer, eds., *Explorations in the Anthropology of Religion. Essays in Honour of Jan van Baal,* The Hague, Martinus Nijhoff, 1975.

151

displayed in order for lived-through experiences to emerge from the theoretical constructions; otherwise, the latter might look like the more or less gratuitous products of exercises in logic that owe their persuasiveness solely to virtuosity.

Thus formulated, the question boils down to that of the relationship between structural analysis and history. Between separate myths, or between different versions of the same myth, the structural analyst infers logical connections whose terms he distributes among the nodes of a network or on the branches of a tree. In these graphs, some myths or variants of myths are allotted a dominant position, others a subordinate one. How far, and to what degree do these hierarchical relations imply a temporal succession? From the fact that one myth seems logically derived from another, does it follow that it appeared after it? And, in that case, how did the succession really occur? Beyond conjectural and implicit history—to which I would have had recourse had I been postulating that the general diagram of logical connections permitting the interpretation of a group of myths repeats, at least approximately, their genesis—I am asked to reach for and dismantle the concrete mechanisms that, on the local level and at a precise point in the history of each group, result in the syntheses which I am accused of aiming at too hastily.

To those objections, it would be legitimate but deceiving to reply that the short-run and localized history of a people without writing eludes us by definition. Rather than return a constat of default, structural analysis will be better served if it watches out for opportunities, even though they may be rare, to document the concrete conjectures from which a mythic transformation has sprung. This is what I should like to try with an American example borrowed from the Salish linguistic (and in large measure also cultural) family, whose representatives occupied in North America a territory extending practically uninterrupted from the Rocky Mountains to the Pacific Coast, between the 46th and 54th parallels, that is, an area corresponding to the northern half of the State of Washington and the southern half of British Columbia.

Most Salish groups of the mainland coast and Vancouver Island owned only one type of mask, generally called Swaihwé, whose area of diffusion extended toward the interior as far as about 150 kilometers upstream from the Fraser River delta. It is, moreover, in this eastern zone that the probable origin of the mask situates itself. Several traditions have it springing from the Tait group or "from upriver," the last representatives in the east of those among the Salish collectively named "Stalo," otherwise called the River People.* To the north, the Tait were next-door neighbors of the Thompson, an inland Salish tribe, who did not have the mask. To be more precise, according to Teit's valuable information, the Thompson of the middle Fraser (Utamqt group) who maintained very cordial relations with the Tait,† owned two specimens, both the property of a family originating, in part, from the delta. They had acquired them recently, says Teit, at a time still remembered by his oldest informants.

Yet, despite the relative novelty and very special circumstances of this double acquisition, the southern Thompson knew the Swaihwé mask's origin myth and told it in nearly the same terms as their Stalo neighbors, in fact, their version refers to this explicitly. The Utamqt Thompson trace the origin of the mask back to a time when the delta groups resided upstream, quite close to them.

According to this version, there was once, among the Stalo, a sick boy whose body was covered with swellings and who, tired of suffering, decided to put an end to his life. He wandered aimlessly

---

* See map 1. Hill-Tout called these people Halkomelem—Trans.

† The name of J. A. Teit, our best authority on the Thompson, is not to be confused with that of the Tait, neighbors of the Thompson on the middle Fraser.

in the mountains, got to a lake and threw himself into it. He landed on the roof of a house that stood at the bottom of the water. Hearing the thud of his fall, the inhabitants let him in. First, the hero·saw a woman with a small child; he spat on the child in passing and infected him with his disease. His hosts, who were Water People, summoned a medicine man, but the latter could do nothing for the child. They then called on the one responsible, who, it was thought, held a magic power. He consented to heal his victim in exchange for his own treatment by the Water People, and the two cures worked.

Some time later, the hero wished to go back home. He was led to the open air through a tunnel-like passage full of water that withdrew ahead of his guides, and was promised a reward for the treatment he gave the child. The hero went back to his village and revealed his identity to his folk. The next day he went to meet the Water People to receive the payment for his services. It was a mask whose description corresponds in every detail to that of the Swaihwé mask. The man exhibited the mask by dancing at feasts, and he became an important personage. The mask was passed on to his children, then to their descendants as a privilege of lineage. Descendants who married into the Spuzzum people (in Thompson territory) and their children, too, however, acquired the right to the mask.

Now, in the same section of the Thompson tribe, the southern Utamqt, one finds an origin myth of a mask whose existence (in contrast to the one above) is nowhere attested by the Stalo. In the way of masks, none but the Swaihwé is known to the latter. And yet, the Thompson myth calls the mask Tsatsa'kwé, a word that might come from the delta languages, meaning "fish" or "salmon." Moreover, this myth of origin unfolds near Yale, in Tait country, and it features characters from this tribe. The myth relates that, among them, there lived a disobedient little girl whom her exasperated parents once beat, sprinkled with urine, and threw out. An uncle took her in and hid her. Her conscience-stricken parents searched for her everywhere. In sorrow because of her family's harshness, and shamed by the cruel treatment she had endured, the little girl decided to do away with herself. After wandering in the mountain, she arrived near a lake where many fish were swimming. She sat down to contemplate them; under her very eyes, they changed into small children endowed with very long hair; they came to the surface to smile at her. They were so delightful and seemed so happy that she had an urge to join them, and she threw herself into the waves.

Immediately, a violent wind rose, devastating the country and demolishing her parents' home. The heroine found that she could not sink; she came out of the water and stepped onto the bank. The wind abated instantly. She no longer saw anything or anyone in the lake. But she had become mistress of the wind. She returned to the village, married and had many children. From then on, her story belonged to her family and her descendants, who carved masks representing the Tsatsa'kwé spirits. Certain descendants held mastery over the wind by birthright or by inheritance: they could unleash it at will. Teit claims to have heard this story from an old man who was only half Thompson, and who had himself received the tale from his ancestors in Yale. At Spuzzum, among the Thompson, only he had the right to wear the mask, but he shared his right with his kinsmen in Yale.

Thus, here we have two traditions collected among the Thompson, both of which refer to their neighbors. The first concerns the Swaihwé mask, which is well attested by the groups of the middle and lower Fraser where it still exists today: the museums own numerous old and contemporary specimens. Several versions of the origin myth are also known, having been collected from the same groups (pp. 22–27); apart from a few details, these are similar to the Thompson version, which was obviously borrowed from them. On the other hand, among the Stalo, no object or mythic tradition suggests the existence of the other type of mask, which the Thompson, who are the only narrators of its origin myth, alone attribute to them. It is unlikely that a foreign testimony, which is, after all, unique, could establish the presence of a cultural trait in a population. One is rather tempted to suspect a local innovation which has sprung up in a zone of intense contact and exchange between neighboring people. As if, on this boundary where the mask's usage becomes lost, they had sought to compensate for this weakening by creating or imagining a new mask, which is simultaneously the same and different. This mask may have existed, but no specimen has survived.

One could not, therefore, immediately dismiss another hypothesis: that the enigmatic Tsatsa'kwé mask is simply the Swaihwé, rebaptized of necessity by a lineage that might have adopted it while inverting its origin myth and its ritual function. In that case, we have the explanation for the odd break in continuity which the myth introduces between the withdrawal of the water spirits and the creation of a mask: because of the inversion that generates the second myth (and extends to the latter's description of the Water People), the mask and the spirits no longer resemble one another. It would therefore be understandable if the new myth chose to delay the manufacture of the mask, entrusting this to the heroine's descendants, who are exempted from portraying it from nature. But, in both hypotheses, the Swaihwé mask as it exists among the Stalo retains absolute priority. For, no matter whether the Tsatsa'kwé differs from the Swaihwé by its nature or is merely the echo of it, its derivative character indubitably results from the mythic origin attributed to it, and from the ritual function assigned to it.

Let me start my argument with the myth. It unfolds roughly like the one on the origin of the other mask. In both cases, we are told about a rejected child who wants to drown him- or herself in a lake. The attempt to do so brings the child to the Water People

Wood figure wearing a Swaihwé mask whose lower half is in the shape of a fish
(Museum für Völkerkunde, Berlin)

who confer on it magical powers, symbolized by the masks. Moreover, the Tsatsa'kwé, as its name indicates, is a fish mask. But the Stalo versions of the origin myth of the Swaihwé are almost unanimous in saying that it was fished with a line, and certain specimens even bear the effigy of a fish.

Thus, the two myths have a common architecture. As soon as one examines them in detail, however, one notices that they contradict one another systematically. In one, the child is a boy; in the other, a girl. The boy is afflicted with a physical defect: his illness; the girl has a moral blemish: disobedience. He is tainted from the inside because of the disease that is gnawing him; she, from the outside, when she is sprinkled with urine. Rejected by her parents—whereas her masculine homologue runs away from them voluntarily—the young girl finds assistance and protection with her uncle, a male relative; while most Stalo versions flank the hero with a sister who helps him. In these versions, the Water People represent the ancestors, notably when the hero marries one of their daughters and founds a lineage. And in the Vancouver Island versions (which, as we have seen, are very closely related to those of the mainland coast [pp. 27–34]), the masks actually are the ancestors. On the contrary, the Tsatsa'kwé spirits are very small children; and, whereas upright feathers "representing hair," as the Thompson version says, decorate the Swaihwé mask, the Tsatsa'kẃe children have long flowing manes—black, one might suppose, given the Amerindian physique, and not white like the feathers (the Thompson version specifies swan's feathers) of the other mask. In the myths of the Swaihwé's origin, the hero is swallowed up by the water. In the Tsatsa'kwé origin myth, this same water casts off the heroine, who, once back at the village, marries on the spot (for the mask will remain, in Yale itself, the property of her descendants). This is in double opposition, therefore, to the Stalo myths of the Swaihwé where it is not the main protagonist—male in this case—who gets married, but his sister, and not in the village, but into an outside group.

Kwakiutl earthquake mask with hinged eyelids, shown closed and open (University of British Columbia Museum of Anthropology)

It can be seen that the two types of myths stand in a correlational and oppositional relationship with each other; this is also the case with the ritual functions assigned to the two masks. From the Salish groups of Vancouver Island and the coast to the Southern Kwakiutl (who have borrowed the mask from them and call it Xwéxwé), the Swaihwé is associated with earthquakes, which the dancers have the power to provoke (pp. 20, 40, 48–49, 126). In this way, and in this way only, can the mastery over the wind attributed to the owners of the Tsatsa'kwé mask be explained. Seism and wind are in opposition, since one upsets the earth, the other the air; but the masks are homologous in relation to these elements whose same instability they express. The mistress of the wind is on the atmospheric plane the counterpart of the master of earthquakes on the telluric plane.

This dual relationship of correlation and opposition between wind and earthquake, which has been inferred through hypothetical deduction, can be checked in a more direct way. The inland Salish, notably the Thompson and Bella Coola (who are also Salish, but isolated from their congeners as the result of an ancient migration) imagine the upper world (sky-country) to be a vast plain, without relief or trees and eternally windswept. Thus they put the celestial world, characterized by its flatness, in major opposition to the terrestrial world where, on the contrary, and as their country's geography attests, a tormented landscape prevails. The same opposition between these morphological features exists among the Coast Salish, too; but it is limited to the terrestrial world whose characteristics it defines: smooth marshy land on one side and rugged terrain on the other. But if, in the first conception, the wind is an attribute of the flat sky, in the second, the crumpled surface, which is in opposition to the land devoid of relief and vegetation, is the result of earthquakes. Some myths explain this relationship (p. 128): a woman and her daughter transform themselves, one into a swamp and the other into an earthquake; and it is said of the latter that she "had power to change the earth's surface; she could make it fold." From which it follows that, in Salish thought, wind and earthquake are in fact diametrically opposed, as are the absence or presence of landscape relief, which characterizes the world above or the world below, respectively. Thus, we indirectly come back to the conclusion I had reached after analyzing, from a formal point of view, the transformation whose different states are illustrated separately by the myths of the Swaihwé and Tsatsa'kwé masks.

Let me now examine one last point. According to Teit's aged informants, the introduction of the Swaihwé masks among the Thompson took place in their lifetime (p. 153), that is, at the earliest in the first half of the nineteenth century. I believe I have established that the origin myth of the Tsatsa'kwé mask derives from the Swaihwé's origin myth, which the Thompson borrowed, along with the mask, from the Stalo. The Tsatsa'kwé myth must, therefore, have been elaborated on the spot, subsequent to the Swaihwé borrowing. Hence, we would have here a particularly clear example of a myth collected fifty years, at most, after having been generated by transformation: a historical conjuncture recent enough for us not only to reconstruct it, but also to understand the mechanisms which triggered the whole operation.

One ought, however, to be cautious in such matters. The available native testimonials on the diffusion of the Swaihwé all suggest that the mask, starting from the middle Fraser, arrived on the coast in the last quarter of the eighteenth century. The various chronologies converge, but should one give them full credit? They are, in my opinion, as subject to caution as the geographical data given by the same informants when, relating their own version of the origin myth, they specify the place where their ancestors fished for the first mask: Burrard Inlet (at the base of the delta) says one, Kawkawa Lake (near Hope) says another, Harrison Lake (half-way between) says a third, and so on. In the course of a conversation with an informant, I have myself been surprised to hear him base his right to the mask on the shortest and most direct line of descent from a first owner as possible; but, on the other hand, the spot where the latter got the mask varies and, by a curious coincidence, it is always situated in the neighborhood. Whether it be on the spatial or the temporal level, each family claiming a right to the mask places the origin as near as possible; paradoxically, the geographical sites multiply at the same time as the genealogies are shortened. But if, as everything indicates, the mask spread from a sole point of origin, it could not have appeared in several places at the same time. The suggested locations thus seem inadmissible, but this does not necessarily mean that the retraced genealogies are false: each may constitute a branch of a longer genealogy, a common stem, the memory of which has been lost in antiquity, or which was quickly forgotten for fear it might reinforce claims in competition with those being given priority.

Even taking into account probable obliterations, the mechanisms through which a certain type of mask has spread over a vast territory by inheritance, marriage, conquest, or borrowing remain visible. One can therefore see how, by being articulated with them, other mechanisms invert the image of the first mask at the point where its propagation loses impetus, just before coming to a halt. The example which I have briefly discussed, in homage to a scientist who never thought that structural analysis was incompatible with ethnohistorical investigations, shows at least how the transformation of a myth could occur in real life.

13

The Social Organization
of the Kwakiutl*

In Part I of this book, I referred briefly to the social organization
of the Kwakiutl and mentioned that it poses very complex problems (p. 92). Today, when the traditional institutions have in
large part disintegrated, observers who attempt to understand their
nature have nothing but old testimonials at their disposal. By its
hesitations and changes of mind, the work of Franz Boas, to which
we owe the essence of our knowledge about the Kwakiutl, brings
out these difficulties well.

Established on the northwest part of Vancouver Island and on
the mainland coast facing it, the Kwakiutl were divided into local
groups which Boas called "tribes." He noted, in his early studies,
that these tribes were subdivided into smaller formations of the
same type, each comprising a variable number of social units which
he called "gens." In contrast with their northern neighbors (the
Tsimshian, Haida, and Tlingit), who are all matrilineal, the
Kwakiutl have a patrilineal orientation and attest, in this regard,

---

*Original version: "Nobles sauvages" in *Culture, science et développement: Mé-
langes en l'honneur de Charles Morazé*. Toulouse, Privat, 1979. A few changes and
additions have been made.

to certain affinities with the Salish-speaking peoples who are their southern neighbors.

But difficulties arise immediately, as Boas was fully aware. First, it is impossible to assert, as the theory of unilineal systems would have it, that the "gens" are exogamous, since each individual considers himself, in part, a member of his father's and, in part, of his mother's gens. Moreover, matrilineal aspects persist because, among the aristocrats—the Kwakiutl forming a stratified society—the husband assumes the name and the arms (in the heraldic sense) of his father-in-law, and thus becomes a member of his wife's lineage. Both name and arms pass on to his children; the daughters keep them, the sons lose them when they marry and adopt those of their wives. Consequently, in practice, the emblems of nobility are transmitted through the female line, and each bachelor receives those of his mother. But other facts work in the opposite direction: it is the father who is the head of the family, not the mother's brother; and above all, authority over the "gens" is passed on from father to son. At the end of the nineteenth century, several individuals of noble birth claimed titles inherited from both lines.

These uncertainties explain why, on second thought, Boas should have changed his perspective and his terminology, as illustrated by *Indianische Sagen* (1895) and his great work on Kwakiutl social organization and secret societies (1897). Until then, he had compared the Kwakiutl mainly to the matrilineal peoples who follow them along the coast, to the north; thus, his first impression was that, from a base of common (i.e., matrilineal) institutions, the Kwakiutl evolved in a patrilineal direction. A few years later, reinforced by new observations, Boas became more impressed by the similarities between the social organization of the Kwakiutl and that of the Salish to the east and south. In both cases, the basic units of social structure seem shaped by a supposed descent from a mythic ancestor who built his home in a definite place, even if this village community later left its ancestral land to unite with other communities of a similar type, without, however, losing the memory of its origin. But, the Salish are patrilineal, and Boas was constrained to invert his initial hypothesis. He now believed that the Kwakiutl, originally patrilineal like the Salish, had partly evolved toward a matrilineal organization upon coming into contact with their northern neighbors. He therefore called the subdivision of the tribe "sept," in the original sense of the term, which in ancient Ireland designated a bilateral group of kin, and he renounced "gens" in favor of "clan," the better to indicate the present matrilineal coloration of this latter type of grouping. These clans, he emphasized, may describe themselves in three ways: some bear a collective name derived from that of the founder; some are called after their place of origin; and lastly, some adopt an honorific name such as "The Rich," "The Great," "The Chiefs," "Those Who Receive First" (at potlatches), "Those Under Whom the Ground Shakes," etc.

Clarifying his previous points, Boas specified that at the time of her marriage "the woman brings as a dower her father's position and privileges to her husband, who, however, is not allowed to use them himself, but acquires them for the use of his son. As the woman's father, on his part, has acquired his privileges in the same manner through his mother, a purely female law of descent is secured, although only through the medium of the husband." That this hybrid law attests to the anteriority of the patrilineal regime, and not the other way around, as he had first thought, Boas found confirmed in several facts: the sister's son does not succeed his uncle; residence is never uxori- or matrilocal; last, and above all, the traditional legends see, in the patrilineal descent of the first male ancestor, the origin of the clans and the tribes, as opposed to the matrilineal peoples of the north who give this role to descent from sisters.

Neither Durkheim nor Mauss, who discussed Boas' interpretations in 1898–99 and 1905–6, respectively, nor Murdock fifty years later, accepted the hypothesis that a matrilineal regime could directly replace a patrilineal regime. It fell on Goodenough (1976) to demonstrate it. But, for French scholars at least, the fundamentally matrilineal nature of Kwakiutl institutions was never in doubt; disagreeing with Boas, they maintained that these were based on uterine filiation. Had not Boas insisted, since 1895–97, on the existence in noble families of a double rule of succession?—from father to eldest child (be it a son or a daughter), but also through marriage, from the wife's father to the son-in-law, and through the latter to the children to come from the union. Furthermore, this second method of succession was of such great importance to the Kwakiutl, that an individual desirous of "entering a house" where there was no marriageable daughter, would symbolically marry a son, and failing a son, a part of the body (arm or leg) of the house chief, or even a piece of furniture.

An important article by Boas, published in 1920, marks a new turning point in his thought. He had, in the interval, trained and enlisted the assistance of an exceptionally gifted informant: George Hunt, son of a Scottish father and a Tlingit mother, but born, raised, and married among Kwakiutl. A model investigator, Hunt collected through the years thousands of pages of information about Kwakiutl culture, from the good housewife's cooking recipes to the dynastic traditions of noble lineages, from techniques of craftsmanship to myths. But these materials, edited and published by Boas in 1921, forced him to reinterpret his data. It was obvious, first of all, that rather than the tribe or the sept, the fundamental unit of Kwakiutl society was the one Boas had first called "gens," then "clan," according to which aspect, patrilineal or matrilineal, seemed predominant in it. "After much hesitation," he renounced these terms and resigned himself to using the indigenous name *numaym* because "the characteristics of the unit are so peculiar that the terms 'gens' or 'clan' or even 'sib' would be misleading."

In fact, Hunt asserted categorically and repeatedly that all the noble genealogies he had collected confirmed that Kwakiutl nobles "never change their names from the beginning, when the first human beings existed in the world; for names cannot go out of the family of the head chiefs of the *numayms,* only to the eldest one of the children of the head chief. And the names cannot be given to the husband of the daughter, none of the whole number of names, beginning with the ten months child's name until he takes the name of his father, the name of the head chief. These are called the 'myth names.' "

Among the dozen names (that is, titles) that a Kwakiutl noble acquires in his lifetime, some—the most important—thus remain the property of the lineage. As for the others: "the only names of the head chief of the *numaym* that can be given in marriage are the names which he obtains in marriage from his father-in-law, and also the privileges, for he cannot give his own privileges to his son-in-law." It seems, therefore, that titles of nobility were divided into two categories: those that could not leave the lineage and were transmitted from father to son or daughter by right of primogeniture, and those that the son-in-law received from his father-in-law through the intermediary of his wife, but to be passed on to their children. These two categories (which, however, the Kwakiutl denied were by nature different) recall, on the one hand, as Boas remarked, *mutatis mutandis,* European majorates and, on the other, the transmission of family heirlooms, which are in theory the property of a lineage, but which are handed down from mother to daughter when the latter marries.

It has been said that the names and privileges mentioned by Hunt essentially constitute titles of nobility. They in fact imply the exclusive use of figured emblems comparable to coats of arms and, also, mottoes, dances, offices in secret societies (according to Boas' terminology, discussed by Mauss): brotherhoods, which—from the beginning to the end of the winter, the ritual season—

replaced the lay organization in force during the other half of the year.

The riches of the *numaym,* however, were not exclusively of a spiritual order. In addition to objects such as masks, headdresses, paintings, sculptures, ceremonial dishes, etc., they included a landed estate made up of hunting and gathering territories, streams, fishing sites, and the locations of weirs (which are also used for fishing). These territorial rights were fiercely defended: their legitimate owners did not hesitate to kill trespassers.

Finally, in his 1920 article, Boas completed his documentation on marriage. Exogamy prevailed in the *numaym,* as was illustrated by the warlike symbolism of the matrimonial rites; but one also finds clear cases of endogamy, for instance, between half-brother and half-sister born to different mothers, and between the father's oldest brother and his niece. According to Hunt, "It is expressly stated that these marriages were intended to prevent the privileges from going out of the family." But it could also happen that, in the absence of a son, the son-in-law, husband of an only daughter, succeeded his father-in-law at the head of the latter's *numaym.* The man in question thus changed his *numaym.* If he had many sons, he sent some back to his original *numaym* to succeed him there, and he kept some with him, to ensure the perpetuation of their mother's *numaym.* More generally, in the case of a marriage between spouses of equal rank, the children could be parcelled out among the maternal and paternal *numaym,* and even, it seems, among those of the grand- or great-grandparents; but each individual kept his freedom of choice, so that affiliation to a *numaym,* while theoretically governed by agnatic law, in real life came closer to a cognatic system of succession.

Until his death in 1942, Boas never stopped thinking about the Kwakiutl and working on the materials gathered in the course of twelve successive visits, spread out over half a century. Brought out in 1966, his unpublished texts give us his last conception of the *numaym* (or of the *numayma* as it is now called): "It might seem that the *numayma* as here described are analogous to the sibs, clans, or gentes of other tribes, but their peculiar constitution makes these terms inapplicable. The *numayma* is neither strictly patrilineal nor matrilineal, and within certain limits, a child may be assigned to any one of the lines from which he or she is descended, by bequest even to unrelated lines." What is, then, a *numayma*? "The structure of the *numayma* is best understood," wrote Boas, "if we disregard the living individuals and rather consider the *numayma* as consisting of a certain number of positions to each of which belong a name, a 'seat' or 'standing place,' that means rank, and privileges. Their number is limited, and they form a ranked nobility. . . . These names and seats are the skeleton of the *numayma,* and individuals, in the course of their lives, may occupy various positions and with these take the names belonging to them."

And yet, one cannot help feeling that in this last state of Boas' thought, the matrilineal features make a strong comeback, in spite of the repeated assertion of a patrilineal predominance. We already know from Hunt that half-siblings born of the same father could marry each other, but not those born of the same mother. Boas goes on to say that to the question, "whose child are you or is he?," the answer always is the name of the mother. The father-in-law proclaims that by marrying his daughter, his son-in-law "comes into his *numaym.*" The witnesses at the wedding say in chorus: "Now (the son-in-law) goes into (the bride's) father's house, that the greatness of (the husband's) name may be increased." And so, after Boas' death and in a period when the traditional institutions have almost completely disappeared, the question of their patrilineal or matrilineal nature remains; as does that of the coexistence of the two principles, assuming they occur simultaneously (but then, what are their modalities?). It is understandable that Boas gave up trying to include the *numayma* in a typology of social

organization. After rejecting all the categories known to him because none was relevant, he could not offer a definition of the
numayma, and resigned himself to describing it as a type of structure without equivalent in the archives of ethnology.

But this equivalent does exist outside America, notably in Polynesia and Indonesia, in Melanesia, and even in Africa, although
for the past twenty-five years, in all their studies devoted to systems spoken of as non-unilineal (and which would better be called
undifferentiated, so as to distinguish them from bilateral systems
which are unilineal, but duplicated),* ethnologists have not recognized it for what it is. One can see two reasons for this.

First of all, this type of institution does not fit with any of the
three modes of descent—unilineal, bilineal, undifferentiated—
which more often than not are treated as separate categories,
whereas institutions of the *numayma* type cut across them.

To check this, it is necessary that the geographical area where
the Kwakiutl are established be examined more closely. Their immediate neighbors, Nootka and Bella Coola, have the same institutions, which, as with the Kwakiutl, are accompanied by a so-
called Hawaiian kinship system (where siblings and cousins are
designated by the same term) and an undifferentiated law of descent. In fact, almost nothing distinguishes the Bella Coola *minmints*
from the *numayma* as described among the Kwakiutl.

---

*In a bilateral or ambilateral system, always well-defined elements of per-
sonal status are transmitted, some down the paternal line, others down the
maternal line. By contrast, an undifferentiated system is one where, according to
the case, and sometimes according to the choice of each individual concerned
or his ascendants, any element of status is transmitted down any one or other
of the two lines. Among the Kwakiutl, if the elements of status transmitted by
agnatic succession and by marriage, respectively, were different in nature, the
system would be bilateral. The present state of documentation does not allow
us to settle the question.

If one goes a little further northward, however, everything seems to change. The Tsimshian have an Iroquois-type kinship system, that of the Haida and the Tlingit resembles the Crow type, and the three tribes are frankly matrilineal. And yet, in the three cases, the basic units of social structure do not have the homogeneous composition one would expect to find under a regime of unilineal descent. Among the Tsimshian, rather than units, we have aggregates formed around a dominant lineage, and others subordinate to it without necessarily having ties of kinship with it. Among the Haida and the Tlingit, the hybrid character of the property laws is the result of various factors: abandonment of ancient lands and acquisition of new ones by occupation or usage, concession of land to immigrants, transfer of titles in compensation for murders or other damages, annexation by neighbors of rights or titles left without heirs, etc.

How can very strictly formulated rules of descent and succession be applied so loosely? The question does not arise in the case of the Kwakiutl, the Nootka, and the Bella Bella, who fully exploit (and even more than that, when one thinks of the sham-marriages of the Kwakiutl) the flexibility of their cognatic system, and can thus disguise all sorts of socio-political maneuvers under the veneer of kinship. By contrast, the rules of the Tsimshian, the Haida, and the Tlingit seem at first too rigid to allow one to shift from one plane to the other; furthermore, the role of kinship proper is more limited, and consequently, the combinations inspired by other motives can be seen more openly. In both cases, the local life inextricably meshes the ties that result from political and economic history, or which it itself creates, with the ties that are based on real or supposed genealogies.

A small coastal population from the north of California, the Yurok, offers another example of the way a unilineal rule of descent disintegrates, if one may say so, upon contact with institutions of the type under consideration. Contrary to the Tsimshian, the Haida, and the Tlingit, the Yurok are patrilineal. But Kroeber, who has studied them assiduously (they hold a place in his work almost comparable to that held by the Kwakiutl in Boas'), emphasizes that "a group of kinsmen is not a circumscribed group, as a clan or village community or tribe would be. It shades out in all directions, and integrates into innumerable others." Among the Yurok, "kinship, accordingly, operated in at least some measure bilaterally and consequently diffusely; so that a definite unit of kinsmen acting as a group capable of constituted social action did not exist."

It is striking that Kroeber pays attention only to the negative aspects of such a situation. The Yurok, he writes, have "no society as such, . . . no social organization. . . . Government being wanting, there is no authority. . . . The men (called chiefs) are individuals whose wealth, and their ability to retain and employ it, have clustered about them an aggregation of kinsmen, followers, and semi-dependents to whom they dispense assistance and protection. . . . Such familiar terms as 'tribe,' 'village community,' 'chief,' 'government,' 'clan,' can therefore be used with reference to the Yurok only after extreme care . . . in their current senses, they are wholly inapplicable."

It is difficult to imagine that a human collectivity, endowed with a language and a culture of its own, could be invertebrate to this degree. But, in reality, the institutions that support Yurok society do exist: they are, first of all, the fifty-four "towns" among which the population distributed itself; and, above all, within each town, the "houses." At last, the word is out; the same word, as a matter of fact, as the Yurok use to designate these, in principle perpetual, establishments, each bearing a descriptive name inspired by the location, the topography of the area, the decoration of the facade, the ceremonial function—the name from which is derived that of the one or several owners.

Thus, for example, the master of the house ha'ägonor, in the town of Omen-hipur, is called Ha'ägonors-otsin, and that of the house meitser, in the town of Ko'otep, Ke-meitser. But, in fact, these houses, of which Kroeber considers only the technique of construction and the utilitarian function (he mentions these only in the chapter devoted to the material culture of the Yurok in his *Handbook of the Indians of California;* he ignores their existence as soon as he turns his attention to the social organization), constitute jural entities. All the native texts collected by Kroeber himself or by his indigenous collaborator Robert Spott, establish this beyond doubt. Thus, in connection with the dissolution of a marriage: "A girl from Sä'a was full-married (that is to say, a high bride price was paid) to the house wôgwu in Weitspus." Her husband died, and after some time, she decided to return to her native town with her little girl. "Her people returned the payment made for her, to wôgwu in Weitspus, because they wanted the girl child. But wôgwu would take only part of the payment back, because if they had taken it all the widow's daughter would have been unpaid for, like a känuks or bastard. . . . In the same way, if she had been killed, or if she had killed or injured anyone, the resulting settlement would have been divided between the two houses." In this case, as in all those with which the texts abound, it is not the individuals or the families that act, it is the houses, which are the only subjects of rights and duties. When, at the deathbed of K'e-(t)se'kwetl, from the tsekwetl house of Weitspus, his wife and his niece squabbled over his inheritance, he settled the argument, before expiring, in favor of his niece because, he said, "the things were not his, but belonged to the house tsekwetl."

Whatever scruples one may feel in expressing a doubt, one can still ask oneself if Kroeber was not mistaken to describe the social organization of the Yurok exclusively in terms of the characteristics it lacked. But if there was a fault, it devolves less on this great master than on contemporary ethnology whose institutional arsenal did not offer the concept of house in addition to that of tribe, village, clan, and lineage.

Secondly, in order to recognize the house, it would have been necessary for ethnologists to look toward history, that of medieval Europe of course, but also that of Japan of the Heian and following periods, that of ancient Greece, and many others as well. Confining ourselves to our Middle Ages, there is a striking resemblance between Boas' definition of the Kwakiutl *numayma* and one that comes from the pen of a European medievalist seeking to outline what exactly is a house. After having pointed out that the noble lineage (*Adelsgeschlecht*) does not coincide with the agnatic line and that it is even often devoid of a biological basis, he refuses to see in it anything other than a "spiritual and material heritage, comprising dignity, origins, kinship, names and symbols, position, power and wealth, which once assumed . . . took account of the antiquity and distinction of the other noble lineages." As can be seen, the language of the anthropologist and that of the historian are practically identical. We are, therefore, in the presence of one and the same institution: a corporate body holding an estate made up of both material and immaterial wealth, which perpetuates itself through the transmission of its name, its goods, and its titles down a real or imaginary line, considered legitimate as long as this continuity can express itself in the language of kinship or of affinity and, most often, of both.

In the statement I have just quoted from, Schmid remarks that the origin of medieval houses remains obscure, since, until the eleventh century, each individual was known by a single name. Indeed, simple and non-recurring names would explain little or nothing; but ancient names are sometimes derived from those of ascendants. And, it cannot be excluded that relationships do exist between the various observable modalities of such a procedure and certain variations of the social structure—a good theme for future collaboration between linguists, anthropologists, and historians.

In the Middle Ages, the oldest procedure was perhaps that of a closed combinatorial system, or finite field: parents called Eberhart and Adalhilt named their two children, boy and girl, Adalhart and Eberhilt, respectively. Less than forty years ago, I observed the same procedure in Amazonia, but stretched over three generations. Merovingian or Carolingian names illustrate a looser combinatorial system, because it is more open in its choice and use of morphemes. The Merovingian princes were called, in the usual French transcription, Theobert, Charibert, Childebert, Sigebert, Dagobert: but also Theodoric, Theodebald, etc. In Charlemagne's family, one notes Hiltrude, Himiltrude, Rotrude, Gertrude, Adeltrude, etc.; but, in addition, the initial morpheme Rot- produces Rothaide, Rothilde; the initial morpheme Ger-, Gervinde, Gerberge; and the initial morpheme Adel-, Adelinde, Adelchis, Adelaide, etc. In other words, the same radical can have several suffixes, the same suffix can have several radicals, and the anthroponymic system is capable of engendering new forms by swarming, so to speak, in opposite directions. Closed in one instance, open in the other, it is a combinatorial system. Still surviving in certain families or regions, a third formula features periodic returns: the grandson's name repeats that of the paternal grandfather; or the name of the sister's son, that of the uterine uncle.

Thus, the alternation of the Pépin and Charles names among the first Carolingians, as a general rule from paternal grandfather to grandson, but the second Pépin, successor of his uterine uncle, was the son of the daughter of Pépin, the founder of the line. The three formulas I have distinguished do not at all constitute an evolving series: they may occasionally coexist in time. And all three of them can be found also among the Indians from whom I have drawn my examples. The Kwakiutl use two types of combinatorial system, closed and open; their expression "to cut the name in two" stands for a mixed form. As for the periodic form, it is observable among the Tsimshian who believed in the reincarnation of the grandfather in the person of the grandson.

It is true that the European kinship systems are neither of the

Hawaiian type like that of the Kwakiutl, nor of the Iroquois type like that of the Tsimshian, nor of the Crow type like those of the Haida and the Tlingit. It is usual to link up the European systems with the Eskimo type, which is characterized by the presence of different terms to designate siblings on the one hand and cousins on the other. I must observe, however, that though the ancient French system does make this distinction, it also brings cousins and kin who are further removed under the same label. As the first meaning of the word cousin, Littré still writes: "Said of all relatives or in-laws other than those who have a special name," an assimilation comparable to that which the Hawaiian systems make between siblings and cousins, except that it is shifted one notch. Apart from this, it allows the same freedom to disguise social or political maneuvers under the mantle of kinship.

All these European medieval houses exhibit the often paradoxical traits which, when found among the Kwakiutl, used to embarass Boas, and which, with regard to other populations, continue to embarrass anthropologists. Let me take them one by one.

Just like its Indian counterpart, the European house possesses an estate consisting of immaterial as well as material wealth. The chief of the house is rich, sometimes immensely so, as Montesquieu observed when he analyzed Charlemagne's will; and in any case, rich enough for his fortune to constitute a political tool and a means of government. To paraphrase Girart de Roussillon: Gifts are his towers and his battlements. The wealth of the house also includes names, titles, and hereditary prerogatives—what used to be called "honours"—to which must be added, as with the Indians, goods of supernatural origin: Saint Martin's cloak, the Holy Ampulla, Saint Denis' banner, the crown of thorns, etc. Outside France, we have Constantine's holy lance, Saint Stephen's crown; or again, in the absence of the objects themselves, the memory of them: thus the grail and the lance of Arthurian legends, which

Glastonbury Abbey pushed to the fore in order to enhance the Plantagenets' prestige.

Let me now consider fictitious kinship; ancient France did not deny itself recourse to this either. Chroniclers, writing probably by command, claimed Carolingian descent for the Capetians, on the highly whimsical ground that Henri I's maternal grandmother's first husband had been Louis V, the last Carolingian, who died without an heir. In the eleventh century, Louis of Provence presumed to Carolingian ancestry, not so much because his mother belonged to this lineage as on account of his being Charles the Fat's adopted son. And everyone knows the role played during the Hundred Years War by Charles VI and Isabella of Bavaria's adoption of Edward V to the detriment of their son, the future Charles VII.

The existence, among the Kwakiutl, of a line of descent going from the grandfather to the grandchildren, through the intermediary of the daughter and her husband, has fueled unending discussions among anthropologists. But, this type of succession seems to have been quite frequent in old Europe where, on many occasions, the question arose of deciding if women could "faire le pont et la planche," that is to say, if they had a son, transmit to him rights which they themselves were unable to exercise (except in the case of female fiefdoms, which, as their name indicates, a woman could inherit). I have just mentioned Edward V's adoption; it was based, among other things, on the fact that his great-grandfather Edward II, being the son-in-law of Philip the Fair, could have acceded to the French throne in case of a succession *per uxorem*. As late as the sixteenth century, Montaigne made fun of the importance his contemporaries attached to the detailed representation of coats of arms, because "a son-in-law will take it to another family."

Innumerable, in fact, were the marriage contracts that gave the son-in-law the right, but also the obligation, to assume, in order to transmit them to his children, the arms of his father-in-law who had no male heir. As early as the eleventh century, the legend arose that the last Carolingian, Louis V, who died in 987, had bequeathed his wife or his daughter to the first Capetian king. In Scotland, in Brittany, in the Maine and Anjou, the daughter inherited the titles in default of a son; the *incoming husband* (or son-in-law) assumed them *jure uxoris* upon "coming into the house," which is the very expression used by the Kwakiutl. It was Henri I's wish that the French crown should pass on to his brother-in-law Baldwin of Flanders, if the legitimate heir, Philip I, died in infancy; in that event, the Count of Flanders, son-in-law of Robert the Pious, would have become the heir *per uxorem*.

Boas had been struck by the fact that in spite of their patrilineal orientation, the Kwakiutl gave the mother's name in reply to the question: whose child are you, or is he? (p. 169). In an interesting article, D. Herlihy notes and comments on the not-insignificant place allotted to the matronym, instead of the patronym, in medieval European legal texts. In view of the general nature of the phenomenon, the regional and historical causes he advances do not seem absolutely convincing. Just like those Kwakiutl nobles who laid claim to titles inherited from both lines, the Capetians busied themselves with acquiring a Carolingian ancestry both from the paternal and the maternal side, but they could only achieve this in three steps: first, by claiming a fictitious kinship; then, using the maternal line alone, through Louis VII's marriage with a descendant of the Carolingians who became the mother of Philip Augustus; but it was only after the latter, in his turn, had married a Carolingian that he could finally bequeath the dual ancestry to his son Louis VIII.

As is the case with the Kwakiutl, the Nootka, and the Bella Coola, for a long time the more prestigious of the two lines was pushed ahead of the other. Schmid cites the case of a lord named Gerold, the biological ancestor of the house, who had a son Ulrich and a daughter Hildegard; yet the documents never mention Geroldingern. It was Ulrich, and not his father, who founded a house, that of the Udalrichingern, doubtless because of the prestige earned through his sister's marriage to Charlemagne. Thus, the house was born from his connection with the Carolingians. But it was the brother, and not the sister, who gave it its name.

As it gained ascendancy, the patrilineal principle stiffled the ancient tendency to ponder the respective advantages of the two lines and to maintain them in balance. But vestiges of this survive in popular usages. In the Languedoc–Provence region, and perhaps also elsewhere, to this day people strive to preserve a relative symmetry between the two lines. At Bouzigues, a small town in the Hérault department, the father's father's name is given to the eldest son, the mother's father's name to the younger son; and, symmetrically, the mother's mother's name goes to the eldest daughter, and that of the father's mother to the younger daughter. The mirror effect is even more striking if one considers spiritual kinship: the father's father and the mother's mother are godfather and godmother of the eldest son and daughter; the mother's father and the father's mother are those of the younger children. On the other hand, a surname is sometimes added to the name, but only the inhabitants of the village have a right to it. That is to say, in addition to the paternal-maternal duality, one must make room for the one prevailing between "countrymen" and outsiders.

This second form of dualism is already visible in the barbarian laws, which, in the matter of succession, reflect a persisting competition of variable degrees of intensity, it must be said, between direct and collateral lines, on the one hand, and on the other, the *vicini;* this term evokes a jural statute whose rules specify the mode of acquisition (Salic Law, title XLV). The dualism of filiation and residence is also brought about by the simultaneous existence of what, even in connection with the Kwakiutl *numayma,* one may call, as in ancient Europe, "noms de race" (ancestral names) and "noms de terre" (territorial names).

During the Middle Ages, it seems that cognatic or agnatic descendants of an illustrious ancestor took a name derived from his: *Leitname* in German. The territorial name was added later, and the old appellation filled the function of collective first name. Toward the twelfth and thirteenth centuries began the custom of members of the same family giving themselves the name of their landholdings and castles; one assumed the name upon receiving the inheritance, which could be maternal as well as paternal. The territorial names consequently became the true names at the same time as the residence's character as center of political action asserted itself. The home of a nobleman crystallized into a "noble house" to the extent that it represented the central point from which his power emanated.

We are unable to go back far enough into the Kwakiutl's past to know if the same evolution occurred among them. But, at the time when Boas knew them, the *numayma* identified themselves either by ancestral names, collective terms derived from the mythical founder, or by territorial names referring to the real or supposed place of origin. A third type of appellation, using honorific terms, tended to supplant the other two: a similar evolution, perhaps, as that which in Europe progressively attenuated the geographical connotation of house names—Bourbon, Orléans, Valois, Savoy, Orange, Hanover, etc.—and associated them mainly with values of power, authority, and prestige.

Whether or not we have here a case of convergence, it nevertheless remains that a dialectic of filiation and residence constitutes a common feature, and no doubt a fundamental one, of societies "with houses." In the Philippines, as well as in some regions of Indonesia, and also in several parts of Melanesia and Polynesia, observers have for a long time now indicated the conflicting obligations that result from a dual membership in a group with bilateral descent and in a residential unit: village, hamlet, or what in our administrative terminology, we would call ward or neighborhood.

When the basic units of the social structure are strictly hier-
archic, and when this hierarchy further distinguishes the individual members of each unit according to both the order of birth and
the proximity to the common ancestor, it is clear that matrimonial
alliances contracted internally or externally can only be made between spouses of unequal status.* In such societies, marriage is
therefore unavoidably anisogamic. Their only choice being between hypogamy and hypergamy, in this respect, too, these societies must compound two principles. A veritable treasure-trove of
ethnographic observations published in the seventeenth century by
La Curne de Sainte-Palaye (a memoir, probably written between
1484 and 1491, entitled *Les Honneurs de la cour*) throws a good
light on this aspect. The author is Eleanor of Poitiers, vicountess
of Furnes, daughter of a lady-in-waiting of Isabella of Portugal
who accompanied her mistress when she came to marry Philip the
Good. But, this minutely detailed description of the customs in
force at the court of Burgundy suggests that the French marriage
terminology, as we know it today, may have resulted from a sort
of semantic slippage. In the fifteenth century, the epithets "beau"
and "belle," appended to the kinship term, were used by a person
of superior rank when speaking to someone placed lower in a system that might include direct or collateral kinship, as well as
marriage. When, in 1456, the dauphin, the future Louis XI, re-
belling against his father, sought refuge at the court of Burgundy,
he dubbed the kneeling Philip the Good his "Bel-oncle." "Madame ma soeur" and "Belle-soeur" were the respective terms by
which close kin addressed each other if they had contracted unequal marriages.

---

*"*L'Astrée* is a romance of the nobility. . . . The first question one nobleman asks another when they meet always was and remains: 'To which house, to
which family do you belong?' According to the reply, he is assigned a deter-
mined place in the hierarchy."

It is therefore only because of the either hypergamic or hypogamic nature of the marriage that these terms were applied mainly to relations between in-laws. The duke of Burgundy, John the Fearless, kneeled in front of his daughter-in-law Michèle of France and called her "Madame"; she answered him with "Beau-père." Similarly, Philip the Good and his wife Isabella addressed their daughter-in-law Catherine, Charles VII's daughter, as "Madame," and she called them "Beau-père" and "Belle-mère." Sainte-Palaye noted, however, that this manner which two interlocutors had of indicating their respective status was permitted, and even prescribed, only in the higher ranks of the nobility: kings and queens, princes and princesses, dukes and duchesses; it was forbidden to houses of lower standing "such as Countesses, Viscountesses, Baronesses, of which there are a great number in several kingdoms and countries." In addition, "it does not belong (to these houses) to call their relations *Beau-cousins* [sic] or *Belles-cousines,* if not otherwise than my Cousin and my Cousine, and whoever does otherwise than it is said, everyone take notice that this is done through vanity and presumption and must be reckoned as nil, because these things are self-willed, lawless and out of reason."

This explains how the use of "beau" and "belle," which was limited to houses of royal blood or close to the throne, acquired a purely honorific connotation in the eyes of the middle class.* As late as the eighteenth century, Diderot's and d'Alembert's Encyclopedia noted in the entry for "bru" (daughter-in-law) that "belle-fille is of better usage." The original connotation of a relatively inferior status, which was perceptible only to the first users, passed unnoticed by the others and was quickly forgotten.

In societies with "houses," and as opposed to what anthropolo-

---

*In today's French, the epithets "beau" and "belle" are used to designate in-laws; thus, beau-père, belle-soeur, and beau-cousin correspond to father-in-law, sister-in-law, and cousin-in-law, respectively.—Trans.

gists observe elsewhere, the principles of exogamy and endogamy are not mutually exclusive either. As was seen in connection with the Kwakiutl, the exogamous marriage is used to capture titles, the endogamous marriage is used to prevent their leaving the house once they have been acquired. It is therefore good strategy to use the two principles concurrently, according to the time and opportunity, in order to maximize gains and minimize losses.

In the same way, European houses have always blended two practices: that of the distant marriage, and that of the marriage very near. The genealogies offer many examples of close marriages exhibiting all the classic forms known to anthropologists: with the patrilateral or matrilateral cross-cousin; or even, one could almost say, "Australian style," as was the case with Philip the Good and Francis the First, who each married a daughter of the son of a father's father's brother. . . . One also finds examples of generalized exchange, for instance between the Capetian house in its early years, the house of Burgundy and the House of Autun.

On the other hand, the marriage of Charles VIII with Anne of Brittany was, diplomatically speaking, very distant since its aim was to pave the way for the union of Brittany with the crown of France. The marriage contract immediately reestablished the equilibrium by stipulating that in case of her husband's death, the widow would remarry the next occupant of the throne, which is in fact what happened when the Duke of Orléans succeeded his cousin once-removed under the name of Louis XII. The rhythm was reversed in the very next generation: Francis I's rather close first marriage was followed by his distant marriage to Eleanor of Hapsburg, the sister of Charles V.

Among peoples without writing, just as in Europe, political calculations inspire and govern this alternated movement of expansion and contraction of matrimonial alliances. In various places, and in different periods, for reasons that were also political, two other similarly antagonistic principles were also compounded: the hereditary right, and the right bestowed through voting. It was in fact in order to overcome this opposition that the first Capetians systematically had their sons crowned during their lifetime. For they had to secure the consent, even if only tacit, of the dignitaries of the realm to reinforce the still doubtful rights of blood and primogeniture: *jurata fidelitate ab omnibus regni principibus,* as was revealingly written—although in a different context—à propos Henri I's succession. The Kwakiutl and some of their neighbors had an analogous and no less ambiguous system of succession. It was the custom for the father to publicly transfer all his titles to his young son, aged ten or twelve years; this was done in the course of a potlatch, which afforded the opportunity, while it also represented the necessity, of obtaining the collective consent and of neutralizing potential rivals publicly. Deferred in the first case (since the heir will reign only after his father has died), immediate in the other (where the father relinquishes all his titles as soon as he has transmitted them), the formula by which a father makes his son his heir in his lifetime offers, in both cases, the means— probably the only one possible—of overcoming the antinomy be- tween inherited and elective rights.

On all levels of social life, from the family to the state, the house is therefore an institutional creation that permits com- pounding forces which, everywhere else, seem only destined to mutual exclusion because of their contradictory bends. Patrilineal descent and matrilineal descent, filiation and residence, hyper- gamy and hypogamy, close marriage and distant marriage, hered- ity and election: all these notions, which usually allow anthropol- ogists to distinguish the various known types of society, are reunited in the house, as if, in the last analysis, the spirit (in the eighteenth-century sense) of this institution expressed an effort to transcend, in all spheres of collective life, theoretically incompat- ible principles. By putting, so to speak, "two in one," the house accomplishes a sort of inside-out topological reversal, it replaces an internal duality with an external unity. Even women, who are the sensitive point of the whole system, are defined by integrating two parameters: their social status and their physical attraction, one always being capable of counterbalancing the other. In Japan from the tenth to the eleventh centuries, the Fujiwara clan secured its enduring control over public affairs by systematically having its sisters and daughters marry heirs to the imperial throne. In such systems, in fact, skillfully manipulated women play the role of power operators. To the successive marriages of Eleanor of Aquitaine (and of so many persons of her condition and sex) corresponds the Kwakiutl custom of compelling the daughter of high noble rank to enter four successive marriages, each one of which conferred an additional supplementary degree of honorability upon her.

How to explain these very peculiar characteristics of the "house" societies which recur in different parts of the world? To understand them, we must return briefly to the Indian peoples with whom I began my study. Among the Tsimshian and the Tlingit, the grandson could succeed directly to the names and titles of his paternal grandfather, notwithstanding the prevailing matrilineal system of descent. This is because the two societies were divided into exogamous moieties: literally, in the case of the Tlingit; and in practice in the case of the Tsimshian, whose phratries, unequal in prestige, tended to marry two by two. In such systems where agnatic generations alternate, it is normal or at least frequent, for the grandfather and the grandson to reproduce each other with respect to the moiety.

But no symmetry exists between these systems and the one illustrated by the Kwakiutl and medieval European societies, a system which, concurrently with a patrilineal law of succession, made the grandson the direct or indirect heir, according to the case, of his maternal grandfather. Neither the inheritance of the daughter's son nor that of the son-in-law *per uxorem* would be compatible with a rule of unilineal descent. In the maternal as well as the paternal lines, such a rule would preclude any element of personal status from belonging at the same time to a daughter's son and to a mother's father.

To interpret this system, one must therefore have recourse to the hypothesis of a latent conflict between the occupants of certain positions in the social structure. Boas' earliest descriptions are so precise that they leave little doubt that, in the noble houses to which his informants belonged, this tension between lineages, which is the crux of the system, resulted in relative preponderance being given to the maternal house. Among the Bella Coola, whose social organization in other respects too seems to have been very similar to that of the Kwakiutl, the observers agreed: "The brother of a woman (married into a foreign tribe) also bestows names on her children, as further mark of their incorporation into her ancestral family." This relative preponderance of the maternal kinsmen confirms my comment on certain Kwakiutl myths (see p. 89).

But this is never openly acknowledged by the other side: the father, as wife-taker, sees in his son a privileged member of his lineage, just as the maternal grandfather, as wife-giver, sees in his grandson a full member of his own. It is at the intersection of these antithetical perspectives that the house is situated, and perhaps is formed. After which, as in opposite mirrors, the initial tension is reflected throughout all levels of social life; and this also accounts for the structural equivalence that the not purely undifferentiated systems of descent (where a unilineal tendency appears) are bound to establish between the daughter's son and either the son or the uterine nephew.

These seemingly interlocking conflicts, and the always double-edged solutions that the "house" societies find for them, in the last analysis, are the result of the same state of affairs: a situation where political and economic interests, on the verge of invading the social field, have not yet overstepped the "old ties of blood," as Marx and Engels used to say. In order to express and propagate themselves, these interests must inevitably borrow the language of kinship, though it is foreign to them, for none other is available. And inevitably too, they borrow it only to subvert it. The whole function of noble houses, be they European or exotic, implies a fusion of categories which elsewhere are held to be in correlation with and opposition to each other, but here are henceforth treated as interchangeable: descent can substitute for affinity, and affinity for descent. From then on, exchange ceases to be the origin of a cleft whose edges only culture can mend. It too finds its principle of continuity in the natural order, and nothing prevents the substitution of affinity for blood ties whenever the need arises.

Thus, with the "house" societies, we see the formation of a system of rights and obligations whose crisscrossed threads cut through the lines of the network it replaces: what was previously united separates, what was previously separated unites. A crossover takes place between the ties society is supposed to secure and those that men once saw as the work of nature, even if, more often than not, this was an illusion. Thus promoted to the rank of second nature, culture offers history a stage worthy of itself. By gluing together real interests and mythical pedigrees, it procures for the enterprises of the great a starting point endowed with absolute value.

14

Hidden Traces of a Mask*

In the first part of this book, I looked at a mask of unusual style, called Swaihwé, belonging to the Salish of the mainland coast and Vancouver Island in British Columbia, and which the Southern Kwakiutl copied under the name Xwéxwé (chap. 3). There is no known equivalent of this mask further north, that is, among the Tsimshian, the Haida, and the Tlingit; as if, a few hundred kilometers from its putative point of origin, the mask, the myths and rites associated with it, and the social and economic functions fulfilled by it, suddenly found no echo.

This boundary poses a problem, for it cuts in two a vast region whose inhabitants have never ceased borrowing myths, rites, ornamental motifs and objects from each other. These people were great travelers; alone or in groups, they readily exchanged visits. Between the various coast or island peoples of British Columbia and Alaska, there reigned, according to the moment or the occasion, sometimes hostility or war, sometimes peaceful relations. In the latter case, the tribes sent out and returned invitations, engaged

*The original version of this chapter appeared under the title "Les Dessous d'un masque" in *L'Homme, revue française d'anthropologie*, 1977, 17 (1):5–27. A few changes and additions have been made.

in commercial exchanges, concluded matrimonial alliances. Nothing happening in the midst of one could remain unknown to the others for long, even if they were distant. It would therefore seem surprising that as considerable a cultural complex as the one which centered on the Swaihwé or Xwéxwé mask would have left no traces in any of the groups, even if they do not offer direct proof of the mask's existence; or, if you prefer—for the two hypotheses are admissible at the start—that we should not be able to perceive the relics of a common stock from which the Salish and the Kwakiutl would have drawn the elements of myth, rites, and plastic works forming this organized whole.

In fact, it is quite probable that such a common stock exists in the north. Even if the Swaihwé mask's trail is not easily discernible, several precise indications allow us to follow it all the way to Alaska. But it is with those nearest to the Kwakiutl, that is to say, among the Tsimshian, that I should fittingly start my quest. These Indians have a myth one episode of which seems so completely out of context that a superficial look might lead us to take it for an interpolation, due to the narrator's whim or to some confusion in his mind. Here it is.

Once upon a time, between two neighboring islands where the coast people went to hunt the sea otter, they often saw a child floating. It was so beautiful that the hunters could not resist the urge to take it aboard. Then, a marine monster called Hakulaq would come to the surface shouting: "Who stole my child, my only child?" He unleashed a frightful tempest, the water submerged the land and the hunters perished, drowned on the island where they had taken refuge. After some time, the only survivors left in the village were a young chief, a woman with her daughter and her two sons—the niece and nephews of the chief—and two other boys who were also his nephews. After several setbacks, they together succeeded in building a solid sea-worthy canoe, went

Housefront painting of the monster Hakulaq flanked by his Killerwhale slaves an

into the ocean, captured the floating child, and disembarked on one of the islands. The infuriated monster caused the island to roll over, but the little team had time to climb back into their canoe, which was left stranded right in the middle of the island when the waters receded. And as the island was upside down, its aspect was that of a steep rock from which one could not escape.

Days went by, and the supernatural child, whom the people had kept with them, died. One night, the chief's eldest nephew raped his own sister. The next morning, she affixed the fur of a

with the heads of children forming his crown (Smithsonian Institution, MNH 2240)

white weasel behind the culprit's head, which transformed him into a male sawbill duck. This is probably the hooded sawbill or merganser (*Lophodytes cucullatus* Linn.) whose "adult male in winter and breeding has the head and neck black with a large triangle of white extending backward from behind the eye. . . ." When the days the young chief had counted were at an end, helped by his nephews, he managed to slide the canoe down a rock and set it afloat again. On the way back, they came upon the sleeping monster, hauled it onto their vessel, escaped a maelstrom provoked by their prisoner, and arrived at their village; there, the monster, in its turn, died. They then went to another village, apparently allied to theirs. There the chief and the three remaining nephews took wives, and his niece also married. The remains of the floating child were one of the wedding gifts. As for the remains of the monster—a female—the hero of the adventure added them to his coat of arms.

World mythology abounds with tales of victories over monsters, and this theme is no less frequent in the myths of the region with which I am dealing. But what is the incest story doing here? None of the preceding episodes anticipates it, and as soon as it is told, it no longer plays the least role in the tale. Of course, incest, too, is a widespread theme; but in this particular case, it presents a double and bizarre inversion when compared with its other American instances. In the myths illustrating what might be called the American Vulgate, a young girl receives the (always nocturnal) visit of a mysterious lover. To identify him, she marks him on the face with soot and in the morning recognizes her brother. She then

Tlingit housepost depicting a human figure (the incestuous brother) transformed into the moon

transforms herself into the sun, and him into the moon. That is why the moon pursues the sun without meeting it, and has a face blotched with dark spots. But, in the present myth, it is the back of the head which is marked, not the face; moreover, this mark consists of a white, not black, spot. This double twist inflicted upon a tale, which is very common in both Americas, is certainly not without significance.

A variant of the same Tsimshian myth, reported by Barbeau, does not contain the incest episode. Like Boas' version, however, it ends with marriages concluded between two villages, that is to say, the opposite of incestuous unions, the danger of which is also avoided (but how?), by preterition in this case, through the destruction of the monster.

This conclusion—one is tempted to say, this moral—is all the more inescapable since the female monster Hakulaq features in

Headdress showing the sea monster Hakulaq with small figures on its back (Collection of Musée de l'Homme, Paris)

another myth, which I have already mentioned (p. 96) and which, like the one above, evolves around a matrimonial problem. A young chief refused all offers of marriage because he was secretly wedded to the woman of the lake by whom he had a child. The scandal broke when this child, who had been captured by one of the chief's companions and brought to the village, caused the death of all the inhabitants (he gouged out their eyes in order to eat them) except the chief himself and his sister. This put an end to the marriage. Upon taking leave of her spouse, the woman of the lake ordered the two young people to part forever, but promised them they would each command great riches. Then she repaired to the ocean and transformed herself into the monster Hakulaq.

In a seemingly arbitrary fashion, the first myth featured an incestuous, thus too-close, union. On the contrary, this myth has a union which is too remote, contracted with a supernatural creature to the detriment of the more or less distanced marriages which the hero rejects; while in the earlier case, marriages at a good distance, between neighboring villages, did prevent a repetition of unions that would be too close, between brother and sister. This latter type of union represents a very real menace in the second myth where a brother and a sister are the sole survivors of a massacre of their kith and kin, a menace which the future Hakulaq wards off by separating the young people forever: they are ordered to journey, one toward the north and the other toward the south. The woman of the lake had promised the brother beforehand that he would win an immense fortune in gambling; and the sister, that she would become Lady Wealth, a supernatural creature, quite well known elsewhere, who enriches all those who meet her or who hear her child cry (p. 104). But the female monster Hakulaq is the opposite of Lady Wealth. She too has a child whom humans find powerfully alluring, but in this case, the consequences are disastrous. The Barbeau version stresses this correlational and oppositional relationship when it specifies that the otter hunters committed the fatal mistake of thinking that the monster's child was the benevolent divinity's offspring.

The Gitksan of the Upper Skeena are distinguished from the coastal Tsimshian by only slight differences in dialect and other differences pertaining to social organization. They, too, know the monster Hakulaq, but for obvious geographic reasons, they locate it in a lake instead of the ocean. Barbeau, who transcribed its name in the form of Hagwelawrh, Hagwelorh, thinks that the Gitksan borrowed the motif from the estuary groups. Their versions, however, present some original traits. According to them, when the monster appears, two (or several) of its children shoot out from its body. On its back, rests a supernatural object: "the snag-on-the-level-of-the-water-forming-a-reef-above-the-sandbar." A noble house adopted it as emblem following a complicated series of events, including an act of incest between brother and sister, which the informants say is based on historical fact. At this stage of my analysis, therefore, it had better be set aside, even though I will come back to it later (p. 208).

In the first Tsimshian myth I examined, the incest between siblings occurs out of context and, as episode, has no discernible function. By contrast, it plays a central role among the Tlingit. As early as 1838, Veniaminov cited it in two distinct forms. The first does not involve incest proper: ashamed because his sister has a lover, a man dragged her to the sky where they were transformed into the moon and the sun, respectively. In the second form, siblings born from the union of a woman and a dog became incestuous lovers. Full of suspicions, the young woman's other brothers daubed her bed with pitch, which stuck to the culprit's thighs and betrayed him. Transformed into thunder, he left his sister and she plunged into the crater of Mount Edgecumbe, near Sitka, where she became Mistress of Earthquakes (p. 111). Several details, such

as the half-human–half-animal origin of the protagonists, the role of monster slayers attributed to the brothers, the mention of a magic ring, which cuts in half the body of those who lay hands on it and ultimately becomes an atmospheric phenomenon (rainbow, lunar or solar halo), allow me to identify these versions with those collected by Swanton, both of which are richer though unequally developed.

A virgin impregnated by the wood dust fallen from a fire drill gave birth to a hero. When he reached adulthood, he slayed monsters, got married, and bequeathed to his son a magic dog and a shirt made of the spiny skin of a fish, the red scorpaenid (Red Snapper, *Sebastes ruberrimus,* cf. p. 50). His son Ḻakîtcîná* was a malevolent character with supernatural powers, who terrorized his wife and killed his children one after the other. He pretended to fondle them, pressing them against his chest, and the spines from his shirt would pierce them through, or else he would grind their faces against a boulder until they died. At Wrangell, there is a representation of him halfway up a carved post: "wearing a hat and the red snapper coat with which he used to kill his children . . . at the bottom the thunder bird (*xēl̲*) which stands for Ḻq!a-yäk!, son of Ḻakîtcîná." I will now turn my attention to this son and to his brothers.

For indeed, the magic dog had had puppies, four males and one female, which the distraught wife succeeded in changing into hu-

*The initial ɬ is a fricative without equivalent in English.

Far left: *Weneel depicted as a very large head that sticks out of the Skeena River, at Kitwanga village, c. 1915 (National Museums of Canada)*; left: *Tlingit monster-slayer ripping apart a whale, on a totem pole in front of Chief Shake's house, Wrangell, Alaska, c. 1905 (National Museums of Canada, no. 72-9715)*

mans (they already secretly were humans, thus suggesting that, as in many other American myths, the wife had conceived them herself with the help of her dog). Łakîtcînâ did not dare attack his new progeny and preferred to fly out at their mother. Coming to her rescue, the children killed him. Henceforth, they devoted themselves to the destruction of several sea and forest monsters.

Here the two lessons collected by Swanton diverge. According to one, the youngest brother commits incest with his sister. Betrayed by the gum sticking to his body, he changed himself into thunder, which one addresses as "Gummy Thigh," and the sister plunged into the crater of Mount Edgecumbe: "This is why people have ever since been very watchful about their sisters." The other lesson does not speak of incest. It limits itself to saying that the brothers interrupted their monster hunt to compel their sister to observe the taboos of puberty (isolation in a cell, use of a tube to draw up water, wearing of a headdress covering the eyes) and to supply her with the bone needles, sinew thread, and porcupine quills needed for feminine handiwork. Later, and although she was still subject to the prohibitions, they took her on a trip with their mother, not without taking extreme precautions. But, as they were crossing a stream one day, they were almost carried away by the current. The mother gave a shout, and the young girl lifted a small corner of her head covering to see. Immediately, the whole family was turned into stones, which have stood in that spot ever since. In this lesson, therefore, a girl's violation of puberty taboos imposed by her brothers replaces the incest of the other

Right (center): *Łakîtcînâ, a supernatural marine being who killed his children by pressing them against the spines of his red snapper shirt, at Wrangell, Alaska* (courtesy of American Museum of Natural History, no. 46109); far right: *Marine monster Qing, wearing the "flood hat" on which people climbed to avoid drowning when Raven caused the Great Flood* (National Museums of Canada, no. K-81-12)

version. But this incest, which is an even graver transgression of the sexual taboos between brother and sister, will provoke "vigilant precautions," which from now on will protect these same sisters, and hence, give rise to puberty taboos.

The Haida tell the same story with very little variation, keeping the same people and place names. They must, therefore, have borrowed the myth from the Tlingit (to whose language all these names belong) and it will be sufficient to point out a few details. More realistic than the Tlingit versions on the subject of the union of the woman and the dog, the Haida tale emphasizes also that her husband, who wore a tunic made of red scorpaenid skin, was so terrible that no one dared look him in the face. Later, when the young heroes resolved to attack, among other monsters, the Big Eel, which had exterminated their maternal kin, they used their sister as bait four times; with her help, they finally triumphed over the monster. Meanwhile, the young girl had her first period; one of her brothers, who was a shameless character, raped her. The others confined themselves to jeering at him, calling him "brother-in-law." The boys then killed and decapitated a monster, whose father Qing (sometimes identified as "The-One-in-the-Sea") came to claim the head, threatening to make the murderers' village collapse. After some difficulties, the heroes extricated themselves from this dangerous situation. After which they quarreled with a character called North who had become the sister's lover and wanted to make them die of cold. Then, for a while, the youngest of the brothers contracted a marriage, which, in recent Tlingit versions, clearly took place in the sky. Then he set off for new adventures with his brothers. A long time after, they together left their mother, and took their sister along with them for new peregrinations. Although ten years had passed since she had reached puberty, they forbade her to look at them while they swam across a river. She disobeyed, and they all turned into rocks or into mountains.

In the child of the marine monster Qing, who sleeps with its feet on the sea bottom with only the floating hair and face showing above the water, it is easy to recognize the floating child in the Tsimshian myth that I used as my starting point. Here as there, the male or female monster turns up unexpectedly on several occasions to claim its child, or what remains of it. When confronted with a refusal, it attempts to destroy the island where the culprits have sought refuge, or their village, with a cataclysm that in both cases resembles an earthquake.

This being the case, very close attention will be given to another Haida myth where we meet again with the floating child, but at the end of the tale instead of at the beginning. There was once a village by the sea. One day, some mysterious visitors came ashore; they had a magic broad hat thanks to which they could, at will, unleash marine cataclysms. Terrorized, the local population had to surrender a princess whom the chief wanted to marry. The travelers, with their prisoner, took to the open sea for an unknown destination. The young girl's parents were disconsolate, and the mother decided to set off in search of her daughter, accompanied by her husband's chief slave. For years, they ventured over the water, facing great perils, and they finally reached the outer confines of the ocean. They slipped under the rim of a celestial dome that was rising and falling in an incessant movement, and, after clearing this last obstacle, they landed on the shores of the beyond. There they met Property Woman carrying her child (p. 107); she explained to them that the country's king had sequestered the young woman in a cave, and made her lose her mind. As a matter of fact, he was furious because his son had given his parents-in-law, as a wedding gift, the magic headdress which he prized above all things. It will be seen that, in this myth, Property Woman appears at the beginning as an accomplice of humans against the powers of the beyond.

The slave left to reconnoiter, found the captive's cell but failed to get her to react; she behaved like an imbecile. Then he made himself temporarily invisible and entered the abductors' dwelling. The conversations he overheard revealed to him that they were a cannibal people, and that the sovereign would return her sanity to the young woman only in exchange for the precious hat.

The two visitors made their presence known; they were feted, then they returned to their country and related their adventures. It was decided to organize an expedition to liberate the captive, but, at the time of departure, the latter's two brothers disappeared. They soon came back, married: the eldest to Mouse Woman (the customary intermediary, in the myths of this region, between the terrestrial world and the beyond), and the younger one to a creature who impressed in spite of her short stature: she was too powerful to look at, she was a woman who "goes by contraries." Led by Mouse Woman, the expedition reached its destination safely. The travelers were given a showy welcome, and they hastened to fill the house up to the very roof with shells. They had brought enormous quantities of shells because it had been noticed, during the earlier visit, that these people of the beyond used old shells as spoons and that at the sight of new shells they were transported with admiration and covetousness. Finally, the magic headdress, main object of the dispute, was deposited on top of the shell heap.

They went to fetch the king of the country. The ground shook as he approached. His appearance was wonderful as he stood there, and his wide-open eyes were too powerful to look at. The ground started to shake again with each step he took. The younger son's wife was the only one who had enough magic power to sustain his glare. Thus foiled, the frightening personage merely retrieved his hat. The shells were parcelled out, and the cured captive was returned to her parents. The king then started to dance, fell, and broke himself in two at the waist. Eagle feathers escaped from his buttocks and his trunk; then, alternatively from each half of his body, were seen coming out his daughter-in-law's retinue whom he had devoured.

The next day, as they were saying goodbye, the king secretly confided to his daughter-in-law that he intended to be born again from her. As soon as she had given birth to him, she should settle him in a cradle decorated with cumulus clouds. Back at the village, the young woman, indeed, did deliver an extraordinary child: "Something flat stuck out from his eyelids." He was placed in a cradle decorated with clouds, and he was abandoned in the high seas. The cradle and its content changed into a rocky reef. Since then, whenever the latter was seen in the morning surrounded by clouds, food would be plentiful; but if it was visible (meaning, probably, free of clouds) this would be an omen announcing that sickness was about to break out.

Swanton, to whom we owe this myth, indicates that it was the first one he had collected in the Skedans dialect and that the translation shows it. One would naturally like to know more precisely what that thing was that stuck out of the newborn child's eyelids. But, before attempting to elucidate this and a few other points, I should observe that the shorter of the Tlingit versions on the incestuous siblings (p. 198) transforms the guilty brother into thunder, whom one implores: "Let it drive the sickness away" or "Let it go northward." The conclusions of the two myths are therefore linked, except that the main protagonist in one version is visible and brings sickness, and in the other he is audible and takes it away. If we now compare the Tlingit and Haida myths about the incestuous siblings (pp. 200–1), we notice that the North has, as I have just said, a benefic connotation in the first, but a malefic one in the second.*

Together with the shifting of the floating child motif from the beginning (or the middle) to the end of the tale, these two indi-

---

*The malefic personification of the North is the lover of the main protagonist's sister, which refers us back to the Veniaminov version (p. 195), where the hero, shocked because his sister has a lover (probably the same personage in the two cases), transforms himself into the moon.

cations suggest that a relationship of inversion exists between myths about sibling incest and the one I have just summarized. And, as a matter of fact, this last myth has as its central motif the forcible removal of a woman whom her brothers, with the help of strangers they have married, succeed in bringing back to her native country. Moreover, instead of the monster-slaying heroes and their sister turning into rocks, it is the monster over whom the heroes triumph who undergoes this metamorphosis. The two tales, therefore, do proceed along inverted paths.

That is not all. I have just recalled that the child in the myth, who at first floats in his cradle, suddenly changes into an ocean reef, a solid high point rising from the water.* By contrast, according to the Tsimshian myth with which I started, the floating child causes a liquid chasm to form, which swallows up the canoes. But, through an oscillation between these two poles, it does seem that, for these Tsimshian Indians, a marine spirit may also become a reef or an islet.

The Barbeau version of the myth I dealt with at the beginning specifies the location of its plot. It features the Gitrhahla (Gitka-tlah), inhabitants of the coastal islands immediately to the south of the Skeena estuary. It seems that these Indians used to camp on Aristobel Island to hunt the otter further out at sea on two groups of islets, which today are called Big Ganders and Little Ganders, respectively. The native name for Little Ganders is Ne-gun'aks. A big monster in the shape of a marine whirlpool had its abode there. It would lure hunters into the channel, and engulf them and their boats. The Tsimshian, however, say in a myth that the hunters visited the kingdom of a marine spirit called Naguna'ks or Nuguna'ks,† probably identical with the name of the group of islets where, according to Barbeau, a monster dwells. This is all

---

*Or, a point level with the surface of the water, like a shoal.
†"Nuguna'ks (a whale; this word means 'mistaken for water')."

the more probable since the spirit Naguna'ks' guests in the end perished in a marine whirlpool for having disobeyed its instructions. It had lavished gifts on them and endowed them with a magic power over all land game, but on the condition that they never again hurt fish or any other ocean creatures. It is interesting that this story, in which the marine spirit manifests itself under the dual physical guises of an islet and an ocean whirlpool, is, of all those we are examining, the only one that gives the spirit an ambiguous moral nature: on the one hand, master of inexhaustible riches, who, like Lady Wealth, ensures the fortune of its protégés; but, on the other hand, making its favors subject to Draconian conditions, for how could islanders subsist without fishing and hunting at sea? Neither entirely good nor entirely wicked, Naguna'ks appears rather to be a jealous and cantankerous spirit that gives nothing for nothing, and causes those who disobey it to perish. Having said this, we can better understand why Tsimshian mythology, whose richer gamut is stocked with intermediate states spaced between the strong ones we have considered so far, might help us elucidate some of the difficulties of the great Haida myth (pp. 201–3) whose analysis I had interrupted provisionally.

It will be remembered that the Gitksan, though living 200 kilometers from the coast, also know the monster Hakulaq or Hagwelawrh; but they make it lacustrian instead of marine (p. 195). According to them, the monster itself looks like a grizzly bear, but it is seen first emerging from under a snag that forms a reef resting on its back and is flush with the surface of the water.

Overleaf: *Weneel depicted on a housefront painting at Port Simpson in 1884, showing three small figures in each eye (the beak, which was almost twenty feet long, has been removed) (British Columbia Provincial Museum, Victoria)*

The Indians saw it and wanted to drag it to the shore. At first, it eluded them, but they noticed that it was covered with various creatures: children, severed heads, the Thunderbird atop small beings . . . Slowly hauled, the snag then revealed the Weneel-with-the-Big-Eyes, equipped with a long beak; next, the Weneel-with-the-Big-Head whose body remained immersed. Finally, from beneath the snag, the Grizzly-Bear-of-the-Water appeared; the leader of the group gave the snag as an emblem to his companions, members of the Gispwudwada clan.

The informants stress the resemblance between the creature called Weneel and the Thunderbird. Decorated monuments represent Weneel with a bird head, a long nose, and a body adorned with feathers. According to a version of the origin myth, a starving Indian suddenly saw coming out of a lake the Weneel called Big-eyes, which had a large human face. With the help of his family, he cut the monster in two and managed to draw the upper half out of the water. Later, he gave a feast and adopted Big-eyes as emblem. This emblem had the shape of a big human face sur-mounting a body without lower limbs, a mere trunk. Another version has the victors over the Weneel get caught in a rockslide from which they have great trouble extricating themselves.

It must be granted that this Tsimshian Weneel looks singularly like the "king" of the other world, as described in the Haida myth. Both are masters of terrestrial upheavals: seism or landslide, and they imprison their adversaries under rocks or in a cave. They have big eyes, a face imposing in its dimensions and expression; they break into two halves at waist level. Feathers escape from the en-trails of one, while the other's body is covered with them. The king of the beyond becomes an infant floating in a cradle, and ultimately changes into a reef. Preceded by floating children, the Weneel supports a snag forming a reef at water level. In conclu-sion, the texts permit us to treat both as avatars, or an aspect of

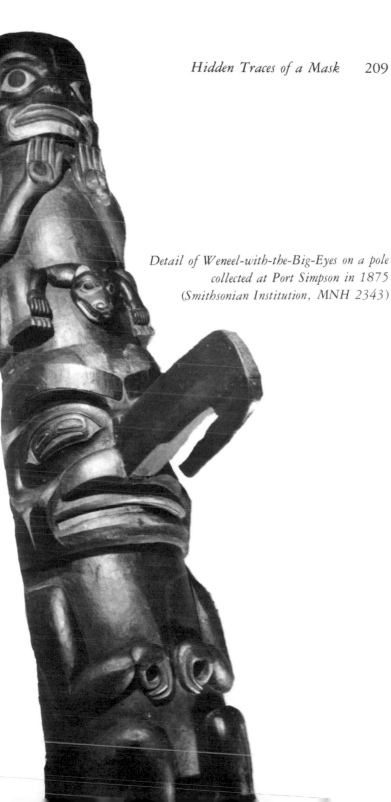

*Detail of Weneel-with-the-Big-Eyes on a pole
collected at Port Simpson in 1875
(Smithsonian Institution, MNH 2343)*

the marine monster called Hakulaq (Hagwelawrh) by the Tsimshian, Qing by the Haida.

On the other hand, while the Haida king of the beyond takes a sister away from her brothers, who will retrieve her only after they have married, the Weneel of the Gitksan and the monster Hakulaq of the Tsimshian have this trait in common: both are associated with an incest story. I have already alluded to this aspect (p. 205), but let us now look at it more closely. Gitksan traditions attribute the capture of the Weneel to a certain Masranaa'o, of whom it is not certain whether he was a historical or a legendary personage. When he was still called Kip-ranaa'o he fell in love with his uterine sister; she gave herself to him. They were both banished, and, for a while, they lived in isolation. Later, they separated. She came back to her village and then concluded a good marriage elsewhere. As for him, the chiefs of a clan different from his own adopted him, a feast was given "to wipe off his shame," and he took a new name. Various actions, rather barbarous but held to be honorable, made him famous; he became a great chief in his adoptive clan. It was while he was suffering from hunger "together with his family, his wife and all" (does this mean his sister, and eventually their children?) near the Nass River, far from his native village, that he got hold of the Weneel and introduced it in his coat of arms.

A contemporary Gitksan memorialist also relates this incest between one Massanal (in whom one recognizes Mas-ranaa'o) and his sister Demdelachu. The events that followed, which conform roughly to those reported by Barbeau, altered the order of precedences in the hero's adoptive clan: he was given first place, and all the dignitaries were set back one notch. As, even today, this protocol is regarded as abnormal, it could be that the incident which gave rise to it had a historical basis. The author relates another incest, however; this one going back to clearly mythical times: also between a brother and sister, both transformed into Thunder-

Weneel shown as a chief's frontlet; abalone shell inlays emphasize the unusual eyes of the creature (National Museums of Canada)

birds, which, at least as far as the brother is concerned, brings us back to the ensemble of myths I have been reviewing.

But it is precisely the ensemble which we must consider now. All the elements of the Swaihwé mask complex are found in it. First, the sociological framework, since the incest motif—whether touched upon, consummated, or avoided—figures in both cases, being opposed to other types of marriages, which are sometimes at good distance, sometimes too far: like the union of a woman and a dog,* or, on another plane, the princess' forced marriage in the beyond. It is therefore significant that, when I was arguing about the Swaihwé mask's origin myth (chap. 2) I should have been led to introduce a critical opposition between the dog and the wife of the main protagonist, while here we have, between the same actors, a relationship that, while no less critical, is one of connection.

In the present mythological ensemble, the rule of avoidance, which imposes itself between brothers and sisters, and the obligation to conclude marriages at good distance, which it generates, occur during or after an exterminating campaign against monsters, the most important of whom is the one (male or female, according to the version) who has a floating child. Implicitly or explicitly, the myths see this monster as a Lady Wealth in reverse. They make it a miser and use various means to bring out this characteristic. Thus, the marine monster Naguna'ks ties unbearable strings to his favors. The king of the beyond, on his part, has recourse to odious blackmail to ensure the return of the wedding gift his son gave his parents-in-law. As has been seen, other myths at first feature a monster that will be destroyed like the rest: a human-looking personage of supernatural origin, who kills children one after the other by pressing them against his tunic, which bristles with spines (see p. 197). This tunic is made of the skin of the red scorpaenid, a fish thought to be monstrous before the father of the said personage killed it, saving the remains, which his son later wore.

*A short Tlingit variant has the heroes born from the union between a human female and the sun. The theme is inverted by the Kwakiutl, for whom the sun's daughter threw her child into the sea near Seymour Narrows, where it became a dangerous current, which takes us back to where we started.

But I have shown (p. 48) that a very close link exists between the Xwéxwé mask and fish of this species, so much so that one might ask oneself whether the very strange appearance of the Swaihwé mask might not be derived from the fish. But furthermore, the main Kwakiutl origin myth of the masks accuses the Scorpaenidae of avarice, and the father in scorpaenid skin is himself miserly and selfish. One version specifies that the reason he kills his children is that he fears they will eat the choicest pieces of the halibut he has caught. In another version, his wife does not dare to eat before he has finished his meal, and she sees to it that her children do the same. One of them, who will be his murderer, challenges the egotist by appropriating his dinner.

Weneel painted on a storage box, with his beak conforming to the corner of the box (British Columbia Provincial Museum, Victoria)

It is therefore not without meaning or consequence that one of the Kwakiutl versions of the lover-dog myth ends with a meal of red snapper. This is an attenuated version, true, since the daughter of a certain village chief, unjustly abandoned by her family for reasons entirely other than a crime of bestiality, survives thanks to the assistance her two dogs give her, as if they were her children. One day, the woman succeeded in catching in her net the son of the marine spirit Komogwa, master of riches, and the young man marries her. When the village chief learned that his daughter was living in plenty, he visited her with two companions. His son-in-law received them with courtesy but offered them, as pittance, only the thin part of a dried fish. It was a red snapper, known even when fresh for having a lean and firm flesh, to which any consumer of it may attest. So, the chief kept for himself alone the minuscule cup of whale oil that his daughter had placed in front of the guests. But the magic cup proved inexhaustible and the chief absorbed so much oil that it leaked from his rectum and inundated the floor: he farted. Ashamed, his daughter had him thrown out.

A Tsimshian myth, also known among neighboring peoples, mentions another character sometimes called Red Cod. He was the slave of the Killerwhales or grampuses, cetaceans who, having carried off the wife of an Indian, proposed to transform her physically into one of their own kind. The husband went in search of her, enlisted the help of the slave and escaped with his wife, while Red Cod blocked the necessary doorways by swelling up his abdomen, thus slowing down the pursuers. It is known that an internal organ of these fish comes up to their mouth and swells when they are pulled out of the water. In relation to the hero, if not to the Killerwhales, the slave's behavior has nothing miserly or frustrating about it. Rather, it allows the reunion of spouses whom fate had set too far apart: this is the reverse problem of that posed by the incest which the real or pretended son of the man in scorpaenid skin will commit.

Tlingit shaman grave with a figure of the shaman holding a red snapper and wearing a red snapper helmet (Smithsonian Institution, MNH 45, 125-H)

This latter personage kills his children; he behaves, therefore, as if he did not want to have descendants. But the Swaihwé origin myths coming from Vancouver Island speak of a woman all of whose children die in infancy and who, through her inability to procreate viable children, prevents her husband—who is the first mask—from founding a lineage. The mainland versions invert this motif, since the hero, once brought back to health, marries the daughter of the chief of the masks for whom he thus secures a line of descent (p. 31). In this respect, in the Haida myth already discussed (pp. 201–3), the king of the beyond behaves in very much the same way as the personage in scorpaenid skin: though he does not, properly speaking, destroy his lineage, he breaks up his son's marriage, which might have given him grandchildren, and he arranges things so as to become his own only descendant, irrevocably fixed at birth in the form of an inert reef. That the king of the beyond and the personage in scorpaenid skin are almost identical is even more clearly brought out in a short Tlingit version where the red snapper coat belongs to a hateful and malevolent shaman, who, like the people of the beyond in the Haida myth, forces the Indians to surrender a young girl to him. The young lady's brothers, who free her, have the same names as the sons of the man in scorpaenid skin of the other myths, one of whom will commit incest with his sister.

Among these myths, those in which the indiscreet sister and her brothers change into rocks or mountains (pp. 198, 200) merely give more extreme expression to the result obtained in other tales by separating the siblings without altering their nature, or by having them marry outside (pp. 190–92, 194, 203–4): whether brothers and sisters remain neighbors, but nailed down to one spot, or separate, in both cases they cannot get together again. In sum, depending on the versions, siblings who are guilty of real or metaphorical incest have only three fates to choose from, two of which are diametrically opposed, while the third occupies an intermediate position. At one end of the axis, one finds thunder and earthquake, in other words, two kinds of turbulence*; at the other end, rocks and mountains, forms of inertia. Equidistant from these two cosmic fates, the third fate, this one sociological, is that of the exogamous marriage which offers the only escape valve to brothers and sisters, who are thereby given a chance to remain human but on condition that each find a spouse elsewhere.

Monsters who are exterminated by heroes can themselves appear in two cosmic forms: the active form of marine turbulence, and the passive form of a visible reef or a rock, flush with the level of the water. Between these extremes, there is an intermediate form illustrated, on the sociological plane, by the spirit Naguna'ks, who pretends to give and take at the same time (p. 205); the spirit Łakîtcîná, who methodically obliterates his descendants (p. 197); and the Haida king of the beyond, who achieves the same result by using a more oblique procedure (pp. 201–3). The myths thus put two codes in a relationship of correspondence: incest and the rejection of or dissatisfaction with procreation, kinds of antisocial behavior, have their equivalent in the natural order where extreme modalities of turbulence and immobility can also be observed.

The myths represent this turbulence in three guises, which we have met in succession: first, the maelstrom, then thunder, finally seism; in other words, tremors affecting the sea, the sky, and the earth, respectively. Thus they have as common denominator the instability of this or that natural element. But, the Swaihwé masks also have command over this instability. Among the Kwakiutl and the Salish, they are masters of the earthquakes; when they appear, muffled rumblings are heard at the bottom of the water and the ground shakes (pp. 20, 27, 40, 47–49, 126, 210). Moreover, like the monsters in the myths I have here examined, and among whom

---

*The Yurok consider Thunder and Earthquake to be two "good companions" who "do the same", one in the sky, the other on earth.

a personage dressed in scorpaenid skin figures prominently, the Xwéxwé masks of the Kwakiutl (closely linked to the Scorpaenidae) are avaricious. While they do not go as far as killing children, as the man in scorpaenid skin does, they are similarly egotistic when they seek to deprive them, if not of food, at least of the gifts meant for them.

Furthermore, the way in which the myths depict the monsters and describe the circumstances of their capture recalls, in all details, what other myths say about the Swaihwé masks. The Tsimshian Weneel and the Haida king of the beyond have enormous eyes, a trait that even inspired one of Weneel's names (p. 208). It is said of the baby who is a reincarnation of the king of the beyond that "something flat" stuck out of his eyelids. This same king had such a powerful stare that no one could look him in the face, just as the personage in scorpaenid skin cannot be looked in the face. Another remarkable trait of the Weneel is a large head; the Swaihwé mask, too, is very big, much bigger than the head of those who wear it.

The Haida king of the other world and the Weneel of the Tsimshian divide themselves in two at waist level. Of the Weneel, only the upper half can be pulled out of the water; this is more or less the same way in which one or several of the Water People, the prototypes of the Swaihwé, abandon their big mask, which was caught like a fish, before going back to the deep. The Haida king of the beyond and his subjects have a passion for shells. The Swaihwé and Xwéxwé dancers carry, as their badge of office, a rattle made of shells threaded on a wooden hoop. An aquatic creature, the Tsimshian Weneel has its body decorated with feathers; and the Haida king—who also, in a sense, is a water creature since he resides in the outer limits of the ocean and one gets to him by boat—produces feathers which spring out of the two halves of his body. The Swaihwé mask offers the same ambiguous character of an aquatic creature—it is fished—whose head and body are decorated with feathers.

In the mainland Salish myths, the hero obtains the mask only with the help and even through the intermediary of his sister. Exiled, the incestuous hero of the Tsimshian myth pulls the We-neel out of the water with the help of his family, then limited to his sister and perhaps their children (though nothing indicates they had any). The most well-developed version of the Haida myth about the personage in the scorpaenid skin asserts that, to capture monsters, the heroes used their sister as bait (p. 200) and that, immediately after, she helped them bring in their catch from the water. Lastly, according to the Tlingit myth on the same theme, the grandfather of these exterminators—who anticipates their work because the monsters he fights are in part the same ones—keeps his victims' tongue: the regular practice of monster slayers, who keep the tongue and sometimes the lower mandible of their victims, in other words, two remarkable features of the Swaihwé mask.

All these considerations bring me back to the Tsimshian myth with which I started, for they suggest a solution to the problem posed by the double inversion we have already observed: that of the black spots on the face—the tell-tale signs of the incestuous brother in what I have called the "American Vulgate"—into a white mark on the back of the head. In one case, the culprit becomes the moon of the blotched face; he becomes the sawbill duck in the other. Could this inversion from black to white, and from the anterior to the posterior part of the head, not be the result of an attempt to transform the incestuous brother of the Tsimshian myth into a sort of equivalent of the Swaihwé mask? For white is the distinguishing color of the feathers that adorn the mask and its costume; and one type of Swaihwé bears the name Sawbill Duck.

Thus, the opposition of white and black, which in the first part of this book had struck me as characteristic mainly of the relation-ship between the Swaihwé or Xwéxwé mask and the ogress Dzo-nokwa, would also be pertinent on another axis. At the two poles of this new axis, there would be, respectively, the black-spotted moon, the offspring of incest, and the white-spotted Swaihwé mask, which affords the means of avoiding it. For this is indeed its role in Salish mythology; and also the role which its assumed equivalent preserves in the Tsimshian myth, where, once the incestuous character has left, his brothers and his sister will find appropriate spouses in another village. Consequently, in all the myths I have analyzed and discussed, the slaying of monsters who share the characteristic traits of the Swaihwé mask permits the opening of an era when, following a more or less harshly penalized act of incest, brothers and sisters will respect the distances that must keep them apart. As another Tsimshian myth specifies (see pp. 193–94), wealth depends on this condition; for its part, the Swaihwé mask, bulwark against incest, ensures wealth to those who own it by birthright or who secure its service.

I believe I have shown that the complex which generated the Swaihwé, far from being restricted to a few Salish and Southern Kwakiutl groups, exists in scarcely veiled form in other coastal populations of British Columbia and Alaska. This already vast area could extend also to the interior, if the Thompson's Tsatsa'kwé, the Lilloet's Säinnux, of which no specimen is known, were the same thing as the Swaihwé. I have tried to establish this for the Thompson elsewhere (see chap. 12). As for the Säinnux mask, it represented a half-human—half-fish monster, and, as with the Swaihwé, white was its dominant color. To which other similarities must be added. The Lilloet origin myth of the Säinnux offers an undoubted kinship with Salish myths on the origin of the Swaihwé. Carved posts, of Lilloet provenance, indubitably represent this latter mask (see p. 35). Lastly, like the Swaihwé masks, the Säinnux masks could not be worn by their owners because of the danger they entailed. This was the reason why, among the Lilloet, the services of an old man (who did not expect much from

Lilloet houseposts (courtesy of Field Museum of Natural History, Chicago)

life anymore) were hired, while the Coast Salish, probably following the reverse logic, entrusted the same office to a young man,
chosen for his robustness (pp. 23, 27, 43). Archeological research
encourages me to push the frontier even further, all the way to
Shuswap country where some rattles or sistrums made of scallop
shells were found, which go back to the Kamloops phase, that is,
to the seventh and eighth centuries A.D. It will be recalled that
instruments of the same composition are the exclusive attribute of
the Swaihwé and Xwéxwé masks. And the Shuswap believe in a
water spirit whose body had a hairy upper part like that of the
Tsimshian marine monster Hakulaq, which ended in a fish tail;
this spirit had the ability to understand the language of birds.
Most Swaihwé masks are decorated with appendages in the shape
of birds, and the Salish myths give them sometimes a celestial,
sometimes an aquatic, origin.

If the Swaihwé complex was so widespread on the coast and in
the interior, we should not be surprised to meet frequently in the
myths relating to it the motif of the dangerous hoop, of which,
basing my reasoning on different grounds, I have already underlined the recurrence at the two extremities of the area and beyond—from the Tlingit in the north, and by way of the Squamish, the Thompson, and the Shuswap, to the Skokomish of Puget
Sound (pp. 111–15). The myths I have examined here make of
the dangerous hoop one of the means used by monsters to defeat
their adversaries: a shiny ring—thus probably made of copper or
other metal—of the bear over which the hero (who will later commit incest) triumphs in a Tlingit myth; an undefined object, but
one that rolls, according to another; cutting rings made from
stringy vines in a third. True, I have associated this dangerous
hoop with the Swaihwé complex through the intermediary of copper, which does not figure in these last myths, or in the Haida
and Tsimshian ones I mentioned. But this is not quite correct, for
the "contrary woman" of the Haida myth, who alone can stand up

to the king of the other world, wears a copper blanket. She is appropriately contrary, however, and in all those versions where the Swaihwé shows through the filigree, we are, so to speak, on the other side of the copper: humans can only hope to acquire it from Lady Wealth or from that other master of riches, the marine spirit Komogwa—who is the Bella Coola equivalent of the Tsimshian's jealous spirit and of the Haida's king of the beyond—after they have put all things in good order: in the universe, by the destruction or taming of monsters; and in society, by drawing up and applying vigilant measures to prevent, at the same time, both the kidnapping of daughters and sisters and sexual unions between too-close kin.

The semantic field I have now covered comprises, according to region, various modalities, which can be characterized as follows. In the south, among the island and coastal Salish, perhaps formerly in the interior also, the Swaihwé mask and character fills a positive role in three respects: as a cure for convulsions, i.e., for tremors which, though they only affect the body, correspond to earthquakes, maelstroms, and tempests in the natural world; as an agent of marriage at a good distance, which removes the risk of incest; and as a dispenser of riches.

North of the Salish, the Southern Kwakiutl, on the contrary, attribute to their Xwéxwé mask (the homologue of the Swaihwé) a stinginess in which one can still perceive, in the attenuated form of a moral flaw, the fundamental maleficence of prehistoric monsters. And, side-by-side with the Xwéxwé, they have another mask whose plastic characteristics are its exact opposite, thus attesting its complementarity: that of the ogress Dzonokwa, survivor from the time of monsters, mistress of immense property which she surrenders to humans or which they take away from her, and, we must not forget, patron of girls who are subjected to the rites of puberty (pp. 74–75, 89).

Lastly, among the Tsimshian, the Haida, and the Tlingit, this relationship of complementarity gives way to a genuine antinomy: on the one hand, monsters of cosmic order and (in the social order) incestuous siblings; on the other hand, Lady Wealth (of whom the Kwakiutl's Dzonokwa assumes certain roles without, however, losing her nature as a monster), who is entrusted with a dual function: to prohibit incestuous unions or assist in the restitution of a young girl to her parents, and to enrich those who agree to obey her. But make no mistake about it: in this state of the system, it is the monsters who occupy the front of the stage; Lady Wealth remains in the wings waiting to make her entrance, or else she plays a very discreet role (see pp. 194, 201). The exterminated or neutralized monsters must vanish, incest must be punished or its menace removed, so that universal disorder is done away with, or rather, so that, should it persist, it is henceforth in the reduced and intermittent form of maelstroms, tempests, and earthquakes; so that, in society, well-regulated matrimonial exchanges are established, but—the legendary history of these people attests to this—without protecting them from political and social jolts, which are also unpredictable and spaced.

Thus the concordance of the cosmic code and the sociological code is sustained down to the details. But concordance does not necessarily mean parallelism. Among the Haida and the Tlingit, as well as among the Salish, the two currents of meanings that I have distinguished converge on one point in the tale. This juncture occurs when the young girl receives from her brother a monster's severed head to celebrate her nubility, and, even more explicitly in the myth of the mainland Coast Salish, when her brother hands over to her the Swaihwé mask, which is or represents the head of a supernatural creature. The effect of this gift is to put a distance between the siblings, for it provides the girl with a dowry thanks to which she will be able to marry (pp. 24, 37, 118). This dowry, however, is not only a material good. As if the fundamental law of exogamous marriage puts onto the eternally suspect woman the onus of proving her innocuousness, the trophy she presents to her husband certifies that, before giving their daughter or sister in marriage, her kin took care to cleanse the universe by eliminating or gaining mastery over the monsters, which constituted an obstacle to the advent of a civilized society.

As long as this decisive step, the triumph of culture over nature, is not taken, the monsters governing the universe retain their original character as savage brutes that feed on human flesh, or who imprison a victim after having deprived her, through their magic power, of the strength to move and of the use of her faculties (p. 201). Those are the redoubtable creatures which the Kwakiutl reduce, on the moral level, to the size of small avaricious deities, and which, taken a step further, the Salish domesticate in the shape of the Swaihwé, even going so far, in the inland versions, as to make them the first ancestors, but without taking away from the masks representing them their demoniacal appearance, which is so striking and puzzling at first sight (see chap. 1).

I believe that I have now answered the critics who, at the time of the first publication in French of *La Voie des masques,* objected that the avariciousness I have lent to the Xwéxwé masks rested on insecure foundations. Besides the fact that these foundations are not at all insecure, since the Kwakiutl origin myth of the Xwéxwé mask sets forth this characteristic in very explicit terms, which are, furthermore, corroborated by ritual practices (pp. 45, 47), it is now plain what the profound meaning of the miserliness attributed to the masks is: it is the still very proximate echo, repeated on the social and moral planes, of the noxiousness of prehistoric monsters of which the Xwéxwé is the last avatar, and whose nature the Swaihwé inverts. This kinship is attested by the fact that, among the Kwakiutl, in the absence of a Cannibal dancer—the contemporary incarnation of the vanished monsters—a Xwéxwé mask takes his place.

In distinguishing three states in the system, however, one should be careful not to see in them three alleged stages of a historical development. It would be all the more unwarranted to envisage an evolution from one type to another since, as was pointed out at the beginning of this chapter, the peoples who have served me as example have never ceased, probably for millennia, to be in close contact: archeological findings demonstrate that they have occupied their respective territories since very ancient times. Consequently, independent of the direction in which the mythic representations evolved here and there, each one of these evolutions could not have missed finding echoes abroad, prompting analogous transformations or—by the same reflex action so often observed between close neighbors—opposite transformations. Representations that were different at the start or that, even if they were not, would tend to diversify, very soon influenced each other. So that the states of the system, as they appear at the time when the majority of the myths were collected (at the end of the nineteenth and the beginning of the twentieth centuries) seem to be the result of a section cut across a complex historical flow, to which it would be unwise to assign a privileged direction.

One point seems certain. All the mythology, as well as traditional legends going back to a relatively recent past, attest that, under the name and appearance of the Xwéxwé mask, the Southern Kwakiutl received the Swaihwé from their Salish neighbors. But this entire investigation leads me to the conclusion that the Salish did not invent the Swaihwé out of nothingness. From one end of a vast cultural area to the other lie the scattered pieces of a system to which, by articulating them, the Salish contributed only a coherence of their own vintage: monsters or spirits associated with water, endowed with a large face, with eyes so big and perhaps already bulging that their gaze is unsustainable, with a tongue constituting such a remarkable feature of their physiognomy that their vanquishers keep this organ as a trophy . . . These monsters have a power over the elements that translates itself into maelstroms, tempests, or earthquakes: upheavals to which the myths oppose the, one might say, peaceful atmospheric phenomena of the lunar or solar halo and the rainbow (see p. 195). Finally, everywhere, there emerges a parallelism between these natural disorders and those which attack familial and social life.

The Salish have not only gathered all these themes to create a model for plastic works. They have also made a synthesis of them from the moral point of view, in the shape of supernatural spirits subjected to and even integrated in the social order. It must be noted, too, that in the Swaihwé ritual as it is being revived quite recently, the masks adopt a terrifying behavior toward the spectators; only the women singing in chorus manage to pacify them, and, after several threatening irruptions, to dismiss them. One will recall, in this connection, the decisive role played in the Haida and Tlingit myths by the sister (i.e., the feminine element in a set or a pair of siblings) in the destruction of monsters and, in the mainland Salish myths, in the capture of the Swaihwé mask.

When and where, among the latter Indians, could the mask have appeared? I have stated elsewhere (p. 160) my reservations on the native chronologies according to which the Swaihwé, from a starting point in the middle Fraser, reached the coast in the last quarter of the eighteenth century, and thus came to the Kwakiutl even later. Indeed, each Salish group claiming a right to the mask locates its origin as near as possible to its traditional habitat, so that these short chronologies disagree on the site where the first mask was obtained. As it is not very likely that it was invented in several places at the same time, I said that the temporal elements of these indigenous traditions call for the same careful scrutiny as do their spatial elements.

It is, therefore, more cautious to admit that the first origin of the Swaihwé and even its evolution in the recent past remain obscure. The similarity of form and functions, which I observed in Part I of this book, between this Salish mask and the Tsimshian,

Haida, and Tlingit coppers complicates the problem further. In any case, it does not prompt me to see in these two types of objects yesterday's or even the day before yesterday's creations. Reconsidered in the perspective of the present study, the opinion collected from informants by Waterman (p. 138), according to which a copper reproduces the form of a child resting on the forehead of a marine spirit, might have a wider significance as more than a mere reference to a decorated monument. Because all through my discussion of the origin of the Swaihwé, and by implication of the coppers, I have come upon the motif of the floating child or the child propped up by a water spirit.

As a matter of fact, on the one hand, the marine monster whom the Tlingit call Gonaqadet (see p. 105) might appear in the guise of a copper or have copper colored fur; on the other hand, one or several children often figure at its sides: "On its (a house at Wrangell) front was the 'chief' monster, with the second monster . . . on the right; the monster's 'wife' on the left. Below were painted five monster 'children.' For it was thought that there were many monsters at Gonaqadet's house, including very young ones: 'these other monsters,' says Gonaqadet, 'are not monsters; they are your people. When I killed your people their souls became my children.' Thus, many children could be seen running along its back. Across its front, it was all over like heads and creatures like children ran across the face." Naguna'ks, the Tsimshian's marine monster, also has children. In connection with the Tsatsa'kwé mask, I was able to trace the floating child motif to the Thompson (see p. 155).

Let us hope that new knowledge on the Indian culture of British Columbia and Alaska will one day allow us to steer the investigation in this direction. By gathering scattered threads, I have only tried to reconstruct the backdrop for a stage some two thousand kilometers wide and perhaps three to four hundred kilometers deep, along whose entire stretch the actors of a play for which we do not have the script have left their footprints.

References

References for direct quotations are indicated in boldface

Pages:

3–8   Lévi-Strauss 1943:175–82; 1958:chap. 13

10–12   Barnett 1955:158–59

15–20   Smith 1941:197–211; Barnett 1955:158, 170, 178–79, 159, 163; Curtis 1907–30:IX, 115–16; Hill-Tout 1902:409; Codere 1948:1–18; Duff 1972 (reprint)

20–21   Curtis 1907–30:IX, 37–39; Boas 1891–95:23–27, 85–86

21–24   Elmendorf 1960:**345**; Cline 1938:**228**; Teit 1906:**279**, 291; Morice 1933:640; Hill-Tout 1902:403–4; Codere 1948:**1–18**

24–26   Teit 1912b:272–73; Boas 1894:455; 1891–95:27, 84–85; 1917:132–33; 1910:820; Stern 1934:57–58

26–27   Stern 1934:**113–15**

32–34   Kuipers 1969:**22–23**; Boas 1917:128; Jacobs 1959:370;

Reichard 1947:**178**; Sydow 1924:pl. 18

35–36   Teit 1906:252–53, 272–73, fig. 95; Dawson 1892:36–37; Teit 1912a:343–46

36–38   Haeberlin 1924:**433**, 28–32; Boas 1935a:**71–72**

40–43   Boas 1891–95:141, 154; 1897:497; Lévi-Strauss 1967:346–48 (1973:*402–3*)

45   Stern 1934:57–58; Boas and Hunt 1921:**891–96**, 951–59

46–47   Boas and Hunt 1902–5:**236–39**

47–49   Boas 1935a:**27–32**, **44–45**

47n   Boas 1888:61; 1891–95:203

50–53   Clemens and Wilby 1961:250, 268–69; Barnett 1955:16; Swanton 1905a:241; Boas 1932b:32; 1916:**297** sq., 898–99; 1891–95:298–99

54   Kuipers 1969:84; Hill-Tout 1900:**525**

56–62   Boas 1935b:144–45; 1910:49, 61; Boas and Hunt 1921:**1122**; Boas 1910:490

62–65   Boas 1897:**470–80**; Curtis

1907–30:X, 184–85; Boas
1966:182

65–66   Barnett 1955:170–71, 296–
303; Stern 1934:51; Smith
1940:187; Jilek-Aall 1972;
Boas 1891–95:89

68   Boas 1934

70–71   Boas 1910:116–22; Curtis
1907–30:X, 293–94

71–73   Curtis 1907–30:X, 296–98

73–75   Boas and Hunt 1902–5:86–
93, 103–4; Boas 1910:442–
45; 1935a:69

75   Curtis 1907–30:X, 295–96

76–77   Boas and Hunt 1902–5:431–
36; Boas 1932b:92–105; Lévi-
Strauss 1972b; 1976

77–79   Boas 1897:372; 1891–
95:135; 1909–10:903–13;
Lévi-Strauss 1967:170
(1973:202); 1968:103
(1978:127); 1971:377
(1981:421)

79–80   Boas 1910:39–81

80–81   Boas 1935a:156–73

81   Lévi-Strauss 1972a

82–84   Hawthorn 1967:152–55; Boas
1910:490; Boas and Hunt
1902–5:96; 1905–8:111;
Boas 1935a:70; 1966:307;
Boas and Hunt 1921:816;
1902–5:364, 398; Curtis
1907–30:X, 296

84–88   Ritzenthaler and Parsons
1966:88–91

88–89   Boas and Hunt 1921:699–
702, 1314

89–91   Boas 1897:358–59; Hawthorn 1967:157, fig. 150;
Boas 1966:51–54

94–95   Boas 1896:579; 1897:394;
1891–95:188–89; 1910:468;

1935a:73, 176, 185, 216;
Boas and Hunt 1902–5:79,
83; 1905–8:24, 60–62; Hawthorn 1967:239–40

95   Boas 1910:267–85;
1935a:219–27

95–97   Boas and Hunt 1902–5:60–
86; Boas 1891–95:219–20

97   Swanton 1909:173–74, 292;
1905b:111, 143; Boas
1916:154 sq.; 1891–95:139,
155, 184

100–101 Boas 1888:55; 1891–95:164,
235; 1897:372–74, 394, 462;
1932a:228; Boas and Hunt
1921:862, 1222–48

102   Boas 1932b:67–69; Krause
1956 (reprint):186; Boas
1900:111–14; Boas and Hunt
1902–5:67

103–4   Boas 1891–95:310–11; Swanton 1908a:665; 1905b:299,
316; 1905a:23, 95

104–5   Emmons 1903:330; 1916:25
sq.; Swanton 1909:119, 128,
173; 1905a:146, 258–59;
Boas 1916:822–23, 835, 846;
Institutet . . . 1927:figs.
238, 256, 259, 260; Jones
1914:188–89

105–6   Swanton 1909:119n, 173,
293, 366–68; 1905a:29;
Moziño 1970:27; Jones
1914:163

107–8   Sahagun 1950–63:XII, 68–
70; Boas and Hunt 1902–
5:378–82; Boas 1916:156,
948; Swanton 1909:173–75,
366–68; Roth 1915:242;
McClellan 1963:121–28; Orico 1930:109; Lévi-Strauss
1967:168–69 (1973:199–

200); Hawthorn 1967:253; Barnett 1955:26, 148, 164–65; Boas 1891–95:84; Swanton 1905a:46; Petitot 1888

108–11 Curtis 1907–30:XVIII, 127–28; Petitot 1886:412–23; Morice 1906–10:V, 644–45; Hearne 1795:175–76; Goddard 1917:333–34; 1912:18–19; Lévi-Strauss 1968:368–70 (1978:446–48)

111 Krause 1956 (reprint):183–86; Boas 1891–95:320; Swanton 1909:20

111–12 Hill-Tout 1900:539–41

112–13 Boas 1932a:222; Sapir 1909:308–11; Boas 1917:44

114 Teit 1898:32–34; 1912b:313; 1909:642; Lévi-Strauss 1971:355–56 (1981:398–99)

114 Adamson 1934:369–71

118–19 Swanton 1909:252–61; Boas 1891–95:140

121–22 Boas 1902:137–68; Swanton 1909:169; Boas 1891–95:84, 85, 88–89

127–28 Ouwehand 1964; Salmony 1954; Fraser 1967; Shunsheng Ling 1956; Badner 1966

128–29 Teit 1909:350, 644, 651; Reichard 1947:57–67; Lévi-Strauss 1971:396 (1981:442); Boas and Hunt 1921:175, 608; Boas 1930, pt. 2:242–43; Steedman 1930:508; Teit 1912b:225; Adamson 1934:160, 172, 175

129–31 Golder 1907:290–95; Boas 1901:39–44, 253; de Laguna 1972:I, 259; Emmons 1911:294–98

130n McClellan 1975:573

133–34 Jenness 1924:73; Teit 1909:703; Vincent 1973; Reichel-Dolmatoff 1968:36; Skinner 1913:120; 1915:760; Skinner and Satterlee 1915:362–63; Jones 1917–19, pt. 2:641

135–37 Keithahn 1964:59–78

137–38 Waterman 1932:448–51; Wingert 1949:60 n72

139 Duff 1972:123–26

141–43 Boas 1897:pl. 6, 346; 1890:838; 1891:610; 1897:421; McIlwraith 1948:I, 398–99

147 Rickard 1939; Witthoft and Eyman 1969; Couture and Edwards 1964

153–55 Duff 1972:11, 19, 123–26; Teit 1912b:273 n3, 272–73, 273 n4, 273–74

160 Teit 1898:22; Boas 1900:28; Adamson 1934:160, 172, 175

161–62 Baal 1971:100

163–64 Boas 1890; 1891–95; 1897

165 Boas 1897:330–33, 334

165–66 Durkheim 1969:216–19; Mauss 1969:58; Murdock 1949:190–91; Goodenough 1976; Boas 1920

166–68 Boas 1920:115, 122, 117; Boas and Hunt 1921:823–24, 787, 782

168–70 Boas 1966:51, 50, 52, 60, 62

172–73 Kroeber 1925:21, 3; Spott and Kroeber 1942:144; Kroeber 1976:437; Spott and Kroeber 1942:148; Kroeber 1976:308

174–75 Schmid 1957:56–57, 3; Lévi-Strauss 1955:418 (1973:362); Boas and Hunt 1921:1107

178	Herlihy 1962:89–120
178–80	Boas and Hunt 1921:259; Schmid 1957:10–11; Bromberger 1976; Schmid 1957:13, 52 and passim
181	Sainte-Palaye 1759:II, 171–282
181n	Elias 1974:291
182	Sainte-Palaye 1759:II, 262, 263
183–84	Galopin 1643:6
185–86	Boas 1925:71; Rosman and Rubel 1971:153–54; McIlwraith 1948:124
189–92	Boas 1916:221–25; Godfrey 1966:82
193–94	Barbeau 1961:71–75; Boas 1916:154–58
194–95	Barbeau 1961:75
195	Barbeau 1961:72; 1929:92–93, 106; 1961:75
195–200	Krause 1956:183–85; Swanton 1908b:434 and fig. 110, 432; 1909:25, 22–25, 95–106, 297–98; de Laguna 1972:II, 875–79
200–201	Swanton 1905b:252–61; 1908a:363, 376–82; Boas 1891–95:306
201–3	Swanton 1905b:150–59; 1909:25
203n	Swanton 1905b:258
204n	Swanton 1905b:172 n22; Boas 1891–95:291
204–5	Boas 1891–95:291–92; 1916:285–92; Barbeau 1961:71–72
205–10	Barbeau 1929:92–93, 104, 106, 105 n1, 105, 108, 106, 107; Harris 1974:128–31
212n	Swanton 1909:295–96
212–13	Boas 1891–95:137, 306; 1916:622; Swanton 1909:99; de Laguna 1972:II, 878; Swanton 1905b:253
214	Swanton 1905b:149; Boas 1891–95:181, 309; 1910:245 sq.
214	Krause 1956:190; Curtis 1907–30:XI, 168; Boas 1891–95:55–56, 259–60, 299–300; 1912:147–191; 1916:840, 843–45; Harris 1974:100–4
216	Swanton 1909:297–98; Boas 1891–95:21, 47, 60
216n	Kroeber 1976:176
220–22	Teit 1906:253, 290; 1912a:344–46; 1906:258, 290; Sauger 1968:147–48; Boas 1890:824; 1916:508; Dawson 1892:36–37; Kuipers 1974:236
222–23	Krause 1956:184; Swanton 1909:98; 1905:156; Boas 1891–95:238
223–24	Boas 1916:355–92; Robinson 1962; Swanton 1905b:256; 1909:104
225	Boas 1891–95:268, 270–71
226	Macdonald and Inglis 1975
227	Jilek and Jilek-Aall 1975
228	Waterman 1932; Swanton 1909:104
228	Olson 1967:105, 110, 121; Boas 1916:288–89

Bibliography

Adamson, Thomas
    1934   *Folk-Tales of the Coast Salish.* Memoirs of the American Folk-Lore Society, vol. 27.

Baal, J. van
    1971   *Symbols for Communication: An Introduction to the Anthropological Study of Religion.* Assen: Van Gorcum.

Badner, M.
    1966   "The Protruding Tongue and Related Motifs in the Art Styles of the American Northwest Coast, New Zealand and China," *Wiener Beiträge zur Kulturgeschichte und Linguistik* 15. Wien.

Barbeau, Marius
    1929   *Totem Poles of the Gitksan.* Ottawa: National Museum of Canada (Bulletin no. 61 of the Canada Department of Mines).

    1961   *Tsimshian Myths.* National Museum of Canada, Anthropological Series 51 (Bulletin 174). Ottawa.

Barnett, H. G.
    1955   *The Coast Salish of British Columbia.* University of Oregon Monographs, Studies in Anthropology 4.

Barrett, Samuel. See Ritzenthaler, R., and L. A. Parsons

Boas, Franz
    1888   "Songs and Dances of the Kwakiutl," *Journal of American Folklore* 1.

    1890   *First General Report on the Indians of British Columbia.* Report of the British Association for the Advancement of Science (1889), no. 59, London.

1891   *Second General Report on the Indians of British Columbia.* Report of the British Association for the Advancement of Science (1890), no. 60, London.

1891–95   *Indianische Sagen von der Nord-Pacifischen Küste Amerikas.* Berlin: A. Asher.

1894   *The Indian Tribes of the Lower Fraser River.* Report of the British Association for the Advancement of Science, no. 64.

1896   *Sixth Report on the Indians of British Columbia.* Report of the British Association for the Advancement of Science, no. 66.

1897   *The Social Organization and the Secret Societies of the Kwakiutl Indians.* Report of the U.S. National Museum for 1895. Washington, D.C.

1900   *The Mythology of the Bella Coola.* Memoirs of the American Museum of Natural History, vol. 2.

1901   *Kathlamet Texts.* Bulletin 26, Bureau of American Ethnology. Washington, D.C.

1902   *Tsimshian Texts.* Bulletin 27, Bureau of American Ethnology. Washington, D.C.

1910   *Kwakiutl Tales.* Columbia University Contributions to Anthropology, vol. 2. New York: Columbia University Press.

1912   *Tsimshian Texts (New Series).* Publications of the American Ethnological Society, vol. 3. Leyden: Brill.

1916   *Tsimshian Mythology.* Thirty-first Annual Report, Bureau of American Ethnology (1909–1910). Washington, D.C.

1917   *Folk-Tales of Salishan and Sahaptin Tribes.* Memoirs of the American Folk-Lore Society 11.

1920   "The Social Organization of the Kwakiutl," *American Anthropologist,* N.S., vol. 22.

1925   *Contributions to the Ethnology of the Kwakiutl.* Columbia University Contributions to Anthropology, vol. 3.

1930   *The Religion of the Kwakiutl Indians.* 2 parts. Columbia University Contributions to Anthropology, vol. 10.

1932a   "Current Beliefs of the Kwakiutl Indians," *Journal of American Folklore* 45.

1932b.   *Bella Bella Tales.* Memoirs of the American Folk-Lore Society, vol. 25.

1934   *Geographical Names of the Kwakiutl Indians.* Columbia University Contributions to Anthropology, vol. 20.

1935a   *Kwakiutl Tales, New Series.* Columbia University Contributions to Anthropology, vol. 26.

1935b   *Kwakiutl Culture.* Memoirs of the American Folk-Lore Society, vol. 28.

1966   *Kwakiutl Ethnography.* Edited by Helen Codere. Chicago and London: University of Chicago Press.

Boas, Franz, ed.

1917   *Folk-Tales of Salishan and Sahaptin Tribes.* Memoirs of the American Folk-Lore Society, vol. 11.

Boas, Franz, and George Hunt

1902–5   *Kwakiutl Texts.* Memoirs of the American Museum of Natural History, vol. 5.

1905–8   *Kwakiutl Texts, Second Series.* Memoirs of the American Museum of Natural History, vol. 14.

1921   *Ethnology of the Kwakiutl.* Thirty-fifth Annual Report, Bureau of American Ethnology (1913–14). Washington, D.C.

Bromberger, Charles (with the collaboration of G. Porcell)

1976   "Choix, dation et utilisation des noms propres dans une commune de l'Hérault: Bouzigues," *Le monde alpin et rhodanien,* 1er–2e trimestre.

Clemens, W. A., and G. V. Wilby

1961   *Fishes of the Pacific Coast of Canada.* Fisheries Research Board of Canada, Bulletin 68, 2d ed. Ottawa.

Cline, W., et al.

1938   *The Sinkaietk or Southern Okanagon of Washington.* General Series in Anthropology, ed. Leslie Spier, vol. 6. Menasha, Wis.: American Anthropological Assn.

Codere, Helen

1948   "The Swai'xwe Myth of the Middle Fraser River," *Journal of American Folklore* 61: 239.

Codere, Helen, ed.

1966   *Kwakiutl Ethnography,* by Franz Boas. Chicago and London: University of Chicago Press.

Couture, A., and J. O. Edwards

1964   *Origin of Copper Used by Canadian West Coast Indians in the Manufacture of Ornamental Plaques.* Contributions to Anthropology, 1961–1962, part 2, National Museum of Canada (Bulletin 194). Ottawa.

Curtis, Edward S.
1907–30   *The North American Indian.* 20 vols.

Dawson, G. M.
1892   "Notes on the Shuswap People of British Columbia," *Proceedings and Transactions of the Royal Society of Canada* IX (1891). Montreal.

de Laguna, Frederica
1972   *Under Mount Saint Elias: The History and Culture of the Yakutat Indians.* 3 vols. Smithsonian Contributions to Anthropology, no. 7. Washington, D.C.: Smithsonian Institution.

Duff, Wilson
1952   *The Upper-Stalo Indians of the Fraser Valley, British Columbia.* Victoria, B.C.: British Columbia Provincial Museum. (Reprinted by Indian Education Resources Centre, University of British Columbia, 1972.)

Durkheim, Emile
1969   *Journal Sociologique. Introduction et notes de Jean Duvignaud.* P.U.F. Paris.

Elias, N.
1974   *La Société de cour.* Paris: Gallimard.

Elmendorf, W. W.
1960   *The Structure of Twana Culture.* Research Studies, Monographic Supplement no. 2. Pullman, Wash.: Washington State University.

Emmons, G. T.
1903   *The Chilkat Blanket.* Memoirs of the American Museum of Natural History, vol. 3.
1911   "Native Account of the Meeting between La Pérouse and the Tlingit," *American Anthropologist,* N.S., vol. 13.
1916   *The Whale House of the Chilkat.* Anthropological Papers of the American Museum of Natural History, vol. 19.

Fraser, D., ed.
1967   *Early Chinese Art and the Pacific Basin: A Photographic Exhibition.* New York: Columbia University Press.

Galopin, G., ed.
1643   *Flandria generosa seu compendiosa series genealogiae comitum Flandriae . . . ab anno Domini 792 usque 1212. . . . .* Montibus.

Goddard, E. P.
 1912   *Texts and Analysis of Cold Lake Dialect Chippewyan.* Anthropological Papers of the American Museum of Natural History, vol.
 10 (2).
 1917   *Beaver Texts.* Anthropological Papers of the American Museum of
 Natural History, vol. 10 (5–6).

Godfrey, W. E.
 1966   *The Birds of Canada.* National Museum of Canada, Biological Series 73 (Bulletin 203). Ottawa.

Golder, F. A.
 1907   "Tlingit Myths," *Journal of American Folklore* 20.

Goodenough, W. H.
 1976   "On the Origin of Matrilineal Clans: A "Just So" Story," *Proceedings of the American Philosophical Society,* vol. 120, no. 1. Philadel-
 phia.

Haeberlin, Hermann
 1924   "Mythology of Puget Sound," *Journal of American Folklore* 37.

Harris, Chief K. B.
 1974   *Visitors Who Never Left: The Origin of the People of Damelahamid.*
 Vancouver: University of British Columbia Press.

Hawthorn, Audrey
 1967   *Art of the Kwakiutl Indians and Other Northwest Coast Tribes.* Seattle
 and London: University of Washington Press.
 1979   *Kwakiutl Art.* Seattle and London: University of Washington Press.

Hearne, S.
 1795   *A Journey from Prince of Wales' Fort in Hudson's Bay to the Northern
 Ocean.* London.

Herlihy, D.
 1962   "Land, Family and Women in Continental Europe, 701–1200,"
 Traditio, vol. 18.

Hill-Tout, C.
 1900   *Notes on the Sk.qomic of British Columbia.* Report of the British
 Association for the Advancement of Science, no. 70.
 1902   *Ethnological Studies of the Mainland Halkomelem.* Report of the British Association for the Advancement of Science, no. 72.

Instittutet für Sammenlignende Kulturforskning
 1927   *Primitive Art.* Series B, vol. 8. Oslo.

Jacobs, M.
1959   "Clakamas Chinook Texts," *International Journal of American Linguistics,* 2 vols.
Jenness, D.
1924   *Myths and Traditions from Northern Alaska, etc.* Report of the Canadian Arctic Expedition (1913–1918), vol. 13, part A.
Jilek, W. D., and L. M. Jilek-Aall.
1975   Symbolic Processes in Contemporary Salish Indian Ceremonials. Mimeograph.
Jilek-Aall, L. M.
1972   "What Is a Sasquatch?—Or, the Problematics of Reality Testing," *Canadian Psychiatric Association Journal,* vol. 17.
Jones, L. F.
1914   *A Study of the Thlingets of Alaska.* New York: Fleming H. Revell Co. (New Haven, Conn.: Human Relations Area Files, 1958.)
Jones, W.
1917–19   *Ojibwa Texts.* 2 parts. Publications of the American Ethnological Society, vol. 7.
Keithahn, E. L.
1964   *Origins of the Chief's Copper or Tinneh.* Anthropological Papers of the University of Alaska, vol. 12.
Krause, A.
1885   *Die Tlinkit-Indianer.* Jena. (*The Tlingit Indians,* trans. by Erna Gunther. Seattle: University of Washington Press, 1956.)
Kroeber, A. L.
1925   *Handbook of the Indians of California.* Bureau of American Ethnology, Bulletin 78. Washington, D.C.
1976   *Yurok Myths.* Berkeley: University of California Press.
Kuipers, A. H.
1969   "The Squamish Language: Grammar, Texts, Dictionary," Part II, *Janua Linguarum. Series Practica* 73/2. La Haye, Paris.
1974   "The Shuswap Language: Grammar, Texts, Dictionary," *Janua Linguarum. Series Practica 225.* La Haye, Paris.
Lévi-Strauss, C.
1943   "The Art of the Northwest Coast at the American Museum of Natural History," *Gazette des Beaux-Arts,* pp. 175–82. [Pages 3–8 of this edition are not quoted directly from the article as pub-

lished in 1943, but have been retranslated from a version rewritten by the author for the French edition of *La Voie des masques.*]

1955   *Tristes Tropiques.* Paris: Plon. (English translation, 1973. *Tristes Tropiques.* London: Jonathan Cape; New York: Harper & Row.)

1958   *Anthropologie structurale.* Paris: Plon. (English translation, 1963. *Structural Anthropology.* New York: Basic Books.)

1967   *Mythologiques II. Du Miel aux cendres.* Paris: Plon. (English translation, 1973. *From Honey to Ashes.* London: Jonathan Cape; New York: Harper & Row.)

1968   *Mythologiques III. L'Origine des manières de table.* Paris: Plon. (English translation, 1978. *The Origin of Table Manners.* London: Jonathan Cape; New York: Harper & Row.)

1971   *Mythologiques IV. L'homme nu.* Paris: Plon. (Eng. trans., 1981. *The Naked Man.* London: Jonathan Cape; New York: Harper & Row.)

1972a   "Compte rendu de M. Detienne, les Jardins d'Adonis," *L'homme, revue francaise d'anthropologie* 12(4).

1972b   "Structuralism and Ecology," *Barnard Alumnae,* spring.

1976   "Structuralisme et empirisme," *L'homme, revue francaise d'anthropologie* 16(2–2).

Macdonald, G. F., and R. I. Inglis

1975   *The North Coast Archeological Research Project: A Ten Year Evaluation.* National Museum of Man, Ottawa. Mimeograph.

Mauss, M.

1969   *Oeuvres: Presentation de Victor Karady.* 3 vols. Paris: Editions de Minuit.

McClellan, C.

1963   "Wealth Woman and Frogs among the Tagish Indians," *Anthropos* 58 (1–2).

1975   *My Old People Say: An Ethnographic Survey of Southern Yukon Territory.* National Museums of Canada, Publications in Ethnology, no. 6(2). Ottawa.

McIlwraith, T. F.

1948   *The Bella Coola Indians.* 2 vols. Toronto: University of Toronto Press.

Morice, A. G.

1906–10   "The Great Déné Race," *Anthropos,* t.V.

1933   "Carrier Onomatology," *American Anthropologist* 35

Moziño, Jose Mariano.
   1970   *Noticias de Nutka: An Account of Nootka Sound in 1792.* Trans. and
               ed. Iris Higbie Wilson. Seattle and London: University of Wash-
               ington Press.
Murdock, G. P.
   1949   *Social Structure.* New York: Macmillan.
Olson, R. L.
   1967   *Social Structure and Social Life of the Tlingit in Alaska.* Anthropo-
               logical Records 26. Berkeley and Los Angeles: University of Cali-
               fornia Press.
Orico, O.
   1930   *Mitos amerindios.* 2d ed. Sao Paulo.
Ouwehand, C.
   1964   *Namazu-e and Their Themes: An Interpretative Approach to Some As-
               pects of Japanese Folk Religion.* Leiden.
Petitot, E.
   1886   *Traditions indiennes du Canada nord-ouest.* Paris.
   1888   *La Femme aux métaux: légende nationale des Déné couteaux-jaunes du
               grand lac des esclaves.* Meaux.
Reichard, G. A.
   1947   *An Analysis of Coeur d'Alene Indian Myths.* Memoirs of the Amer-
               ican Folk-Lore Society, vol. 41.
Reichel-Dolmatoff, G.
   1968   *Desana: Simbolismo de los indios Tukano del Vaupés.* Bogotá.
Rickard, T. A.
   1939   "The Use of Iron and Copper by the Indians of British Colum-
               bia," *British Columbia Historical Quarterly* 3.
Ritzenthaler, R., and L. A. Parsons
   1966   *Masks of the Northwest Coast: The Samuel A. Barrett Collection.* Pub-
               lications in Primitive Art, no. 2. Milwaukee Public Museum.
Robinson, W.
   1962   *Men of Medeek: As Told by Walter Wright.* Kitimat: Northern Sen-
               tinel Press.
Rosman, A., and P. Rubel
   1971   *Feasting with Mine Enemy.* New York and London: Columbia Uni-
               versity Press.
Roth, W. E.
   1915   *An Inquiry into the Animism and Folklore of the Guiana Indians.* Thir-

tieth Annual Report, Bureau of American Ethnology (1908–9). Washington, D.C.

Sahagun, B. de
1950–63   *General History of the Things of New Spain: Florentine Codex.* 13 parts. Trans. by A. J. O. Anderson and C. E. Dibble. Santa Fe: School of American Research.

Sainte-Palaye, J. B. de la Curne de
1759   *Mémoires sur l'ancienne chevalerie.* 2 vol. Duchesne. Paris.

Salmony, A.
1954   *Antler and Tongue.* Supplement to *Artibus Asiae.* Ascona.

Sapir, Edward
1909   *Wishram Texts.* Publications of the American Ethnological Society, vol. 2. Leiden.

Sauger, D.
1968   *The Chase Burial Site.* Contributions to Anthropology, no. 6. National Museum of Canada, Anthropological Series 6 (Bulletin 224). Ottawa.

Schmid, K.
1957   "Zur Problematik von Familie, Sippe und Geschlecht, Haus und Dynastie beim mittelalterlichen Adel. Vorfragen zum Thema 'Adel und Herrschaft im Mittelalter.' " *Zeitschrift für die Geschichte des Oberrheins,* vol. 105(1). Karlsruhe: Verlag G. Braun.

Shunsheng Ling
1956   *Human figures with Protruding Tongue, etc.* Bulletin of the Institute of Ethnology, Academia Sinica, vol. 2.

Skinner, A.
1913   *Social Life and Ceremonial Bundles of the Menomini Indians.* Anthropological Papers of the American Museum of Natural History, vol. 13.

1915   *Societies of the Iowa, Kansa and Ponca.* Anthropological Papers of the American Museum of Natural History, vol. 11, part 9.

Skinner, A., and J. V. Satterlee
1915   *Folklore of the Menomini Indians.* Anthropological Papers of the American Museum of Natural History, vol. 13, part 3.

Smith, M. W.
1940   *The Puyallup-Nisqually.* Columbia University Contributions to Anthropology, vol. 32. New York: Columbia University Press.

1941   "The Coast Salish of Puget Sound," *American Anthropologist* 43.

Spott, R., and A. L. Kroeber
    1942   *Yurok Narratives.* Publications in American Archeology and Eth-
            nology, vol. 35, no. 9. Berkeley and Los Angeles: University of
            California Press.

Steedman, E. V.
    1930   *The Ethnobotany of the Thompson Indians.* Forty-fifth Annual Re-
            port, Bureau of American Ethnology (1927–28). Washington,
            D.C.

Stern, B. J.
    1934   *The Lummi Indians of Western Washington.* Columbia University
            Contributions to Anthropology, vol. 17. New York: Columbia
            University Press.

Swanton, John R.
    1905a   *Contributions to the Ethnology of the Haida.* Memoirs of the Ameri-
            can Museum of Natural History, vol. 8, pt. 1.

    1905b   *Haida Texts and Myths.* Bureau of American Ethnology, Bulletin
            29. Washington, D. C.

    1908a   *Haida Texts.* Memoirs of the American Museum of Natural His-
            tory, vol. 14.

    1908b   *Social Conditions, Beliefs and Linguistic Relationship of the Tlingit
            Indians.* Bureau of American Ethnology, Annual Report. Wash-
            ington, D.C.

    1909   *Tlingit Myths and Texts.* Bureau of American Ethnology, Bulletin
            39. Washington, D.C.

Sydow, E. von
    1924   *Ahnenkult und Ahnenbild der Naturvölker.* Berlin.

Teit, J. A.
    1898   *Traditions of the Thompson River Indians.* Memoirs of the American
            Folk-Lore Society, vol. 6.

    1906   *The Lilloet Indians.* Memoirs of the American Museum of Natural
            History, vol. 4.

    1909   *The Shuswap.* Memoirs of the American Museum of Natural His-
            tory, vol. 4.

    1912a   "Traditions of the Lilloet Indians of British Columbia," *Journal of
            American Folklore,* vol. 25.

    1912b   *Mythology of the Thompson Indians.* Memoirs of the American Mu-
            seum of Natural History, vol. 12.

Veniaminov. See Krause, A.

Vincent, S.
1973   "Structure du rituel: la tente tremblante et le concept de mista.pe.w," *Signes et langages des Amériques: Recherches amérindiennes au Quebec* 3:1–2.

Waterman, T. T.
1932   "Some Conundrums of Northwest Coast Art," *American Anthropologist* 25.

Wingert, Paul S.
1949   *American Indian Sculpture: A Study of the Northwest Coast.* New York: J. J. Augustin.

Witthoft, J., and F. Eyman
1969   *Metallurgy of the Tlingit, Dene, and Eskimo Expedition.* Bulletin of the University Museum of the University of Pennsylvania, vol. 2, no. 3.

Index